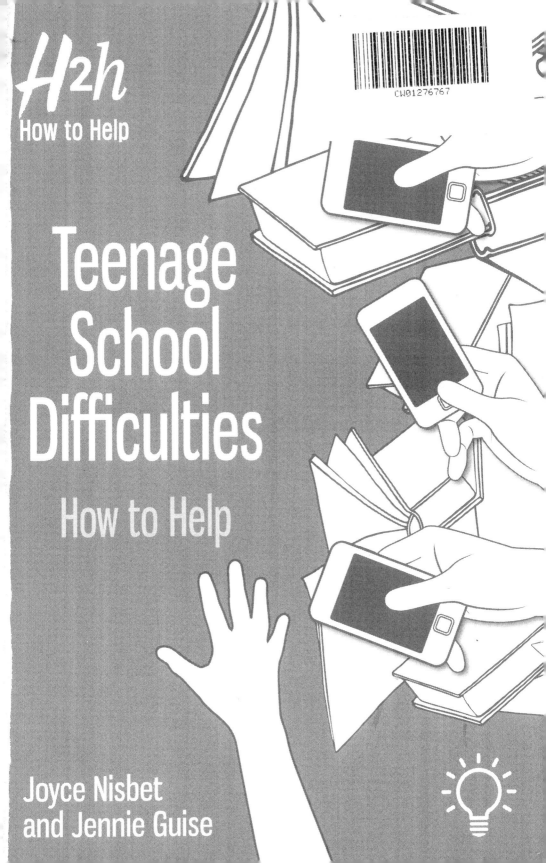

Teenage School Difficulties

© Pavilion Publishing & Media

The authors have asserted their rights in accordance with the Copyright, Designs and Patents Act (1988) to be identified as the authors of this work.

Published by:
Pavilion Publishing and Media Ltd
Blue Sky Offices, 25 Cecil Pashley Way
Shoreham-by-Sea, West Sussex
BN43 5FF

Tel: 01273 434 943
Email: info@pavpub.com
Web: www.pavpub.com

Published 2022

All rights reserved. No part of this publication may be reproduced, stored in a retrieval system, or transmitted in any form or by any means, electronic, mechanical, photocopying, recording or otherwise, without prior permission in writing of the publisher and the copyright owners.

A catalogue record for this book is available from the British Library.

ISBN: 978-1-912755-91-2

Pavilion Publishing and Media is a leading publisher of books, training materials and digital content in mental health, social care and allied fields. Pavilion and its imprints offer must-have knowledge and innovative learning solutions underpinned by sound research and professional values.

Authors: Joyce Nisbet and Jennie Guise
Cover design: Emma Dawe, Pavilion Publishing and Media Ltd
Page layout and typesetting: Emma Dawe, Pavilion Publishing and Media Ltd
Printing: CMP

Contents

Series Preface v
About the Authors vi
Authors' Preface vii
How to Use This Book... ix

Part 1: Introduction 1
Chapter 1: What are teenage school difficulties? 3
Chapter 2: Pastoral Care, Guidance and Alternative Education 9
Chapter 3: Principles, policies and processes 13
Chapter 4: Provisions and collaborations....................................... 17
Ten key things to know about teenage school difficulties 21

Part 2: Primary school and transition issues 23
Chapter 5: Primary school 25
Chapter 6: Teenage transitions 31
Chapter 7: Transitioning to secondary school................................. 37
Chapter 8: Organisation... 43

Part 3: Secondary school and educational issues....................... 47
Chapter 9: Increased workload 49
Chapter 10: Subject choice... 53
Chapter 11: Disengagement 57
Chapter 12: Truancy and absenteeism 65
Chapter 13: School refusal... 71
Chapter 14: Post-school options 75

Part 4: Personal and health issues 79
Chapter 15: Illness and disability 81
Chapter 16: Mental health 85
Chapter 17: Self-esteem.. 89
Chapter 18: Sexual health.. 95
Chapter 19: Eating disorders 101
Chapter 20: Self-harm..109
Chapter 21: Dependency..115

Part 5: Interpersonal issues 123

Chapter 22: Friendships 125
Chapter 23: Bullying 129
Chapter 24: Cyberbullying 135
Chapter 25: Peer pressure 141
Chapter 26: The 'quiet victim' 145
Chapter 27: Separation and divorce 149
Chapter 28: Financial problems 155
Chapter 29: Bereavement and loss 159
Chapter 30: Young carers 163

Part 6: Conclusion 167

Chapter 31 – Summary 169
Chapter 32 – A last word to parents and carers 177
Chapter 33 – A last word to teachers and schools 179
Index of *How to Help* advice 181
Index of case studies 183
References 185

Series Preface

Young people in today's society face considerable stresses. The Prince's Trust, which has monitored youth opinion for ten years, found that just under half of young people who use social media now feel more anxious about their future when they compare themselves to others on websites and apps such as Instagram, Twitter and Facebook. A similar proportion agreed that social media makes them feel 'inadequate'. The *Guardian Weekly* noted in early 2019 that more than half of young people think that social media creates 'overwhelming pressure' to succeed.

There are many issues that are likely to affect every pupil at some point during his or her time at school. How these are dealt with can be 'make or break' for some pupils, because of the crucial stages in education that can be affected. The implications are deep and broad because, understandably, the child's experience of education, and his or her success at school, can have a tremendous impact on later life chances.

The *How to Help* series covers a broad and comprehensive range of topics that will have resonance for today's parents, carers and educators. Each title is designed to make a valuable contribution in the breadth of issues that it introduces, and the realistic helping strategies that it puts forward.

Gavin Reid and Jennie Guise
Series Editors

About the Authors

Joyce Nisbet has extensive experience of teaching across the secondary school age range. She taught History and English in a school with 1,100 pupils, then worked as Principal Teacher of Guidance (Pastoral Care) in a school with 1,700 pupils. She initiated, developed and for more than twenty years led an innovative, highly successful flagship model of alternative education to cater for the varying needs that can arise in a school with 1,300 pupils aged 12-18.

Jennie Guise is a Practitioner Psychologist and author. She has worked in research, and now in applied practice as founder and Director of Dysguise Ltd. Her main interests are in identifying what will help individual learners to progress and in helping to break down, or work around, the many and various barriers that can affect learning. She works collaboratively with educators to apply that knowledge in practical ways.

Authors' Preface

The first author of this book, Joyce Nisbet, has had many years of practical experience in dealing with a whole range of issues that can affect pupils in secondary education. In this book, we draw on this experience and knowledge, and help to make it available and accessible to a wider audience.

In our work, we are both very keen to provide a practical, non-judgemental and accessible perspective on problems that can be overwhelming to those people who are in the thick of them. With that in mind, we have provided simple bullet-point strategies for parents and carers, and for teachers and schools. We believe that it is crucial for parents/carers and teachers/schools to be 'on the same page', working together for the benefit of the pupil, and not pulling in opposite directions. We have used case studies that draw on real situations to illustrate the wide range of issues that we discuss.

While the case studies are based on secondary school pupils, many of the topics (for example issues relating to friendships, bullying, disengagement, divorce and bereavement, and so on) are equally applicable at primary level, and we do separately discuss factors that may be particularly relevant to younger children. Our aim throughout is to provide practical suggestions, based on years of relevant experience at the forefront of best practice in working with pupils across the educational spectrum.

Joyce Nisbet
Jennie Guise

How to Use This Book

Topics in this *How to Help* book are organised within four major sections, comprising Parts 2 to 5:

- Primary school and transition issues
- Secondary school and educational issues
- Personal and health issues
- Interpersonal issues

Within these sections, each topic is discussed in a separate chapter (although it should be noted that in practice there will frequently be areas of overlap), with advice for parents, carers, teachers and schools. You can read through the sections in order or go straight to what concerns you most. The topics have been chosen to represent the key issues that typically comprise the workload of a school pastoral care professional.

We have used case studies to show how a support team can engage with pupils and parents to design a plan of action for each issue. The background to our case studies, and the context from which they are drawn, is described in Part 1.

Whenever you see the *How to Help* icon, you can expect to find practical, ready to use suggestions and strategies for helping children and young people to understand, address and overcome teenage school difficulties.

We recommend that you read in full the Introduction (Part 1) and the Conclusion (Part 6). The former serves as an entry point into the main chapters, presenting the subject and core principles relating to it along with a list of ten essential things to know. The latter summarises the most important points for readers to take away, and offers final comments for parents, carers, teachers and schools.

To keep up to date with the *How to Help* series, bookmark:

www.pavpub.com/howtohelp

"Pooh felt that he ought to say something helpful about it, but didn't quite know what. So he decided to do something helpful instead."

A.A. Milne

Part 1: Introduction

Chapter 1: What are teenage school difficulties?

Introducing teenage school difficulties

Young people, as every parent or carer knows, can encounter all sorts of difficulties during their adolescent years. In this book we will explore those teenage challenges that relate specifically to school and education, and offer advice for parents, carers, teachers and schools on 'how to help'.

> ### Key Point
> *Young people, as every parent or carer knows, can encounter all sorts of difficulties during their adolescent years.*

Literally speaking, 'teenage' should mean aged 13-19 (i.e. any number that ends with 'teen'). However, the definition we will use in this book is somewhat broader. We will focus primarily on the secondary or high school years (including sixth form) which means young people aged 11-18. We'll generally use the term 'secondary school' to describe this context and population, but we acknowledge that it is by no means the only term and you may prefer 'high school', 'senior school' or an equivalent. Likewise, when we talk about 'primary school', this can also mean 'junior school', 'elementary school' or whatever term is most familiar and comfortable for you.

Young people today are schooled in all sorts of environments and contexts (including home schooling), and we have titled this book 'Teenage School Difficulties' precisely because we wish to avoid limiting its scope to any one term, context or approach. Our advice is universal, and we hope our title is too.

The issues and difficulties that young people can experience as they attempt to make their way through secondary education and simultaneously cope with the challenges of adolescence are many and varied. Some of the more obvious ones relate to the initial transition to a bigger school with increased workload, more subjects and teachers, more peers, greater burden of homework and so on. Others may be much more personal to the child – for example mental health issues or family circumstances such as divorce, illness or bereavement. While some of these problems may eventually resolve themselves over time, all are likely to have at least a short-term impact on the happiness, wellbeing and educational performance of the individual. And all are likely to be beyond the young person's emotional experience to resolve by themselves. So it is critical that parents, carers, teachers and schools identify warning signs and provide early support where appropriate.

Notwithstanding our focus on the secondary school years, it is important not to ignore background history. A child's early years, family experience and circumstances all contribute to the emotional health and wellbeing of the young person who walks through the school gates into a new situation – a melting pot of other teenagers, more adults, additional stresses and huge physical and emotional changes. Problems in children are often identified by Health and Community Workers well before primary school age. They can be rooted in family circumstances, child health issues, parent or carer health issues and more. Indeed, there may well be evidence of intervention or concerns before admission to primary school, and these will be entered into the child's PPR (Pupil Progress Report) or equivalent.

When young people are coping with personal issues at school, the playing field becomes less even for them and they can easily lose out. They are already dealing with pressure, so anything that tips the balance can have long-term consequences and effective support is invaluable. Furthermore, how an individual young person deals with difficulties depends very much on their own personality, resilience, support network and relationships with peers and adults in school. This is why, as we will explore in this book, it is essential for schools to treat children and young people as individuals with individual needs, and to work with parents to provide effective, personalised pastoral care.

Pastoral care in schools

Pastoral care is a responsibility of all schools, and it means having provisions in place to ensure the physical and emotional safety and wellbeing of each and every pupil. With good pastoral care in place, all children and young people can flourish and perform to their full potential.

Pastoral care is a core part of every curriculum, taught under headings such as Personal and Social Education (PSE) and Personal, Social and Health Education (PSHE). This of course is a hugely positive development and much to be welcomed. Today's school children have a far more detailed and liberal understanding of issues of health, mental health and wellbeing than their parents or grandparents ever did. And this is important, because it means that for young people struggling with such issues the stigma that once existed is much reduced. This helps them to share their difficulties, open up to those who can help, and receive the individual care and support that they deserve.

Factors affecting performance at school

We have already touched on the fact that a wide range of factors can influence pupils' behaviour (usually with a knock-on effect on attainment) in secondary school. A useful conceptual framework for considering this is provided by the American psychologist Urie Bronfenbrenner (1917-2005) through his 'ecological systems theory' (Bronfenbrenner, 1977)[1]. In Bronfenbrenner's model there are five levels of influence, starting with the individual and moving gradually outward to incorporate bigger and wider social groups.

Bronfenbrenner's levels of influence are presented visually as a set of concentric circles within circles – like a target with the pupil at the bullseye.

The five levels are:

- The individual
- The 'micro-system'
- The 'meso-system'
- The 'exo-system'
- The 'macro-system'

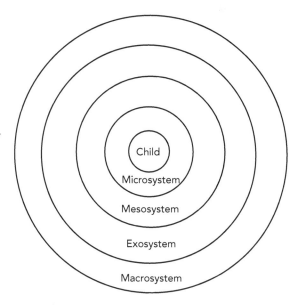

At the individual level, we can consider biological factors such as age, sex and health. Surrounding the pupil, the 'micro-system' includes people known to the pupil – for example, friends and family. Next is the 'meso-system', describing the various connections that exist between elements in the micro-system – for example, how the pupil's family

---

1 Bronfenbrenner, U. (1977) Toward an experimental ecology of human development. American Psychologist, 32 (7): 513-531

relationships affect relationships with friends or teachers. The wider 'exo-system' describes bigger, institutional influences such as the school, the community and neighbourhood and social services. While it is less tangible, this level has an important impact on everything it surrounds. Finally, the 'macro-system' is the most abstract level, and can be described in very general terms as the 'society' or 'culture' within which the pupil lives and learns.

The many influences on a pupil cannot be easily separated out and there will always be overlap, but ecological systems theory can be helpful in encouraging us to systematically consider the various layers, levels and networks that play a part in shaping behaviour.

Core principles of pastoral care and support

High quality pastoral care and support involves a number of fundamental principles:

- Prioritising and promoting the wellbeing of young people
- Working within the Child Protection Guidelines (or local equivalent)
- Putting young people at the centre, and always working towards best outcomes
- Taking a whole-child (pupil-centred) approach to support
- Working closely with parents, carers and families
- Working with teaching staff to effectively manage progress
- Co-ordinating support agencies and other professionals
- Building strengths, and promoting resilience

It is a fact of school life that behaviour management takes up a disproportionate amount of teacher and Senior Management Team time. Methods of dealing with behavioural issues and 'repeat offenders' can result in a revolving door of punishments, disengagement and exclusion from school. Often, an inordinate amount of staff time and energy is taken up, to little immediate or long-term effect. Added to this, other issues often go unaddressed and pupils who are quietly struggling with life are often left to continue quietly struggling. How many pupils underachieve at a crucial point in their lives because of external factors? As adults they might be able to look back and quantify this, but as young people in the here and now they may perhaps drop a few grades, do less well than they (and others) had hoped, and not be able to get into the career or course they wanted. It may never be realised that, with better pastoral care, the bump in the road might have been avoided or at very least minimised.

Providing good quality, practical support for young people is clearly an important investment in their future – and, indeed, in the future of our society. Despite this, it is often the poor relation in terms of funding and a soft target for financial cuts. For this reason, it is a good investment of time for any parent, carer, teacher or school to pay attention to any and all issues that can affect children and young people and have an impact on their education. By maximizing controllable positive factors and minimizing negative ones, we can ensure that each and every one of our young people is in the best possible frame of mind for learning when he or she arrives at school each morning.

Chapter 2: Pastoral Care, Guidance and Alternative Education

The pastoral remit and Guidance

A lesson that all teachers quickly learn once they are put in charge of a classroom is that they don't have a class to teach, but a group of individuals. Each has his or her own story, problems and needs, and these are not constants. Also, teachers don't teach subjects – they teach young people, and the lives of those young people are often on a knife edge because of factors outside school. Pupils often give away details of their home lives when lessons raise group discussion of moral issues. If we think back to our own families and consider the full range of problems, intrigues, tensions and worries that we observed, we can appreciate that teenagers being brought up in similar environments are often fully aware of what is going on around them. They then carry this load each day into their own stressed teenage environment, and it's no wonder that many don't cope at some point.

> **Key Point**
>
> The pastoral remit in education includes personal issues, sex and health education, curricular issues, and liaison with external support agencies.

The pastoral remit in education includes personal issues (family, health, attendance, behaviour), sex and health education (following a structured programme throughout the secondary school years), curricular issues (academic progress, record-keeping, reporting to parents, course choices for national exams), and liaison with all relevant external support agencies. In Scotland, where both authors of this book are based, this remit is encapsulated within the role of Guidance Teacher and, more broadly, the Guidance Department. As well as helping to support young people in school and covering the specific requirements of the post, Guidance work involves dealing with issues for individual pupils as they arise, often as emergency situations.

In Scottish schools, the Guidance Department sits alongside the Learning Support Department, which deals with learning and Specific Learning Difficulty (SpLD) initiatives. It is highly valued by parents and by other members of teaching staff as a practical response to coping with any issues raised for a young person. While the specific Guidance title and role is unique to Scotland, the principles it operates on are universal. For this reason, we will draw extensively on the author Joyce Nisbet's first-hand experience as a Guidance Teacher – and particularly a Guidance Teacher who set up her own 'Alternative Education Department' to provide high quality pastoral care within a city secondary school – as an example of good practice throughout the course of this book. We will use the terms 'pastoral care' and 'Guidance' interchangeably, especially within our case studies.

Learning from experience – about the case studies

As a starting point, we will use this chapter and the next to briefly describe the specialist support provision that Joyce Nisbet, some thirty years ago, put in place in a secondary school in central Scotland. Our reason for doing so is that, while clearly much has changed since then in terms of technology (and this itself poses new risks to the health and wellbeing of children and young people) the underlying principles of good pastoral care have not. In exploring Joyce's work within the school, we will seek to show how these principles were made to operate in practice. For teachers and schools, there may be important insights to take away for your pupils. For parents and carers, we hope that the case studies will provide an inside look at how good schools can and do support young people with difficulties.

We want to be clear that while our case studies are drawn from a particular geographical context, this by no means excludes readers who are based outside Scotland or indeed outside the UK. It is our belief that the way Scotland approaches pastoral care in education has a great deal to offer any parent, carer, teacher or school seeking to find out more about how to help young people with teenage school difficulties. Therefore we will use anonymised examples from Joyce's work throughout this book to show how issues were identified, and how staff engaged with pupils and parents to decide and implement a plan of action. Times and places may change, but the lessons of good pastoral care will always remain valid and relevant to all.

Introducing the Alternative Education Base

When Joyce Nisbet submitted to her central Scotland secondary school a proposal for an 'Alternative Education Department', she had a very clear view of what it should not be. At that time, in the late 1980s, many schools had a 'sin bin' where disruptive pupils were sent for periods of time. These were often staffed on a rota basis, with no single teacher being responsible for the facility or for the wellbeing of the pupils referred there at crisis point. There was little opportunity for a restorative approach. The Alternative Education Department would not be like that. Instead, it would have a positive image among pupils, and would never be seen by anyone as a 'dumping ground' or a punishment.

The 'Base', as it became known, changed and evolved over time. Every encouragement was given by the Head Teacher and Senior Management Team – those who held the purse strings – to expand the range of work and bring in as many outside agency resources as possible, and this was a constant feature of the Base's activity. If a pupil came with a new or very specific problem, staff would not only search for ways to offer in-house support, but would also engage help from specialist agencies who could support a pupil beyond the confines of the school, the school day and even the school term.

As the Base's workload increased, more funding for staff and space was negotiated. At its peak, the department comprised six team members – three Teachers, a Classroom Assistant/Art Specialist, a Youth Strategy Social Worker and a Group Worker. As part of the Senior Management Team's commitment, teachers were hand-picked for the Base. One was a careers officer with a teaching background, known and liked by the school's pupils, whose knowledge of careers and work experience placements proved invaluable. The other had, over time, developed positive relationships with young people in the school, particularly those with behaviour management issues.

The Classroom Assistant/Art Specialist brought creativity and a range of practical skills that engaged pupils in group and individual work and helped to raise confidence and self-esteem. Artwork produced in the Base was displayed throughout the school and sold to raise money for in-house projects and pupil-nominated charities. There was a mixed gender balance. Joyce, as the Base's Head, was always invited to sit on the interview panel for the Youth Workers and Group Workers who were employed to work in the school part-time. She had regular meetings with the Head of the Community Education Department and acted as Line Manager for the school-based Youth Worker. This helped to keep the profile of the Youth Worker post at the forefront for funding, which enhanced relationships between the school and the other community centre staff in the local area.

The room allocation also increased over time until there was a suite of four rooms – a main room (the Base), an office/interview room/staff base, a kitchen, and a room that could be converted into a mini-gym. They were all centrally located in the school, next to the library and with easy access for all pupils and parents. Free rein was given with regard to furnishing and decoration. It incorporated designated soft seating areas, a quiet space, interview facilities and an area where vulnerable pupils could have breaks and lunches in a quieter setting. One room had a medical couch, where pupils could rest or sleep if that is what they needed to do. Lockers were fitted for pupils who required help with organising their day, and who needed to 'drop in' between classes.

The Base was and still is unique in Scotland (and beyond). It was set up to offer a wide-ranging, pupil-centred and innovative approach to supporting young people. Many other schools looked to the Base as a marker for effective support. Visitors came from all over the world to learn about what was viewed as a flagship resource, and advice was frequently sought on the Alternative Education approach to supporting the full range of pupils.

Chapter 3: Principles, policies and processes

Guiding principles of the Alternative Education Base

The underlying principles of the Alternative Education Department, or the 'Base', can broadly be listed and categorised in terms of 1) the fundamental philosophy in working with young people, 2) taking a practical approach to a range of issues, 3) ensuring inclusivity, and 4) supporting staff and parents.

The fundamental philosophy:

- First, do no harm.
- Recognise that young people are individuals, with individual issues.
- Offer a safe environment, a sympathetic ear, and support – always within national child protection guidelines.
- Offer a non-punitive approach to behaviour management that avoids stigma in the school towards those referred to Alternative Education.
- Listen to young people, and offer counselling on an individual basis.
- Keep young people at the centre of the dialogue, and involve them in planned support/provision.

Taking a practical approach to a range of issues:

- Address issues affecting learning, and negotiate a plan of action.
- Challenge poor behaviour, and agree positive plans of action.
- Develop resilience and interpersonal skills.
- Offer 'time out' or cooling-off periods for vulnerable pupils.
- Provide careers advice and negotiate work experience placements for individual pupils.
- Access relevant outside agency provision, on an individual or group basis, to support young people (for those already receiving support from an outside agency, liaise with any named workers after negotiation with the pupil).

- Look for creative, innovative alternative approaches to support young people to remain in the mainstream – including reduced timetables, reduced days and part-time work experience.

Ensuring inclusivity

- Offer a meaningful and personal level of support to any young person disadvantaged by personal issues, whatever his or her academic ability.
- Work with every new pupil enrolled in the school – often from different schools, towns, cities and countries – through an induction programme and 'buddying' system.
- Offer a reduced timetable life skills provision for vulnerable young people, to help them gain self-confidence and to encourage independence and resilience.
- Address classroom behaviour and liaise with staff and Senior Management to avoid exclusions from school.
- Monitor exclusion statistics, and look for causes and effective strategies to reduce exclusions.

Supporting staff and parents

- Involve parents as much as possible in planning and decision-making.
- Offer advice to staff, on a department or individual basis, regarding the management of individual pupils.
- Offer training sessions to newly qualified teachers to make them aware of the work of the Base, and of the issues affecting young people in school.
- Encourage staff to consider creative approaches to their classroom management for individuals.
- Produce an Annual Report, distributed to all school staff and support agencies/partners, to inform them of the work of the Alternative Education Department.

Referral of pupils to Alternative Education

In order for the Alternative Education Base to work effectively, it needed rules, policies and activities that were defined enough to enable manageable operation, but flexible enough that the child could always to be the priority. This began with initial referral into the facility.

Pupils could be referred to the Base by their Guidance Teachers after discussion at a weekly, multi-agency Pupil Support Group meeting, or they could be taken in on the same day as the referral. A simple one-page form was used as the basis for discussion with the Guidance Teacher (who would already have discussed this with the pupil and his or her parents or carers, to explain the role of the Base and to obtain permission for the referral). No pupil would be full-time in the Base for any great length of time, although some would work with the Base at various times during their school career.

Pupils already known to the Base could self-refer using a 'Yellow Card' system at what the pupil might see as a vulnerable time, at a time when he or she might truant or when personal issues made it difficult to be in a classroom. Pupils in the Base's Anger Management Programme were issued with these cards – to be used before a confrontation, or to avoid escalation of anger. Referrals for anger management came from the Pupil Support Group (an inter-agency group that met in school each week to discuss individual cases), who could also refer pupils for one-to-one work with the school Youth Worker.

Referrals for one-to-one work with the Youth Strategy Social Worker came from the Pupil Support Group and from the Working Together (Social Work) team. Emergency referrals to the Base could be made by Guidance or Senior Management staff for any pupil finding it difficult to cope in class, or a pupil facing a personal or family crisis. The Alternative Education Teacher working with the pupil would regularly feed information back to the Guidance Teacher and the Pupil Support Group as required.

A staged process for addressing issues

Staff working within the Alternative Education Department always followed a carefully staged process when working with children with teenage school difficulties. This process was as follows:

- Listen carefully to what the young person has to say. Allow for silences. Don't fill in the gaps, or make assumptions, but use open questioning to encourage dialogue and reflection.
- Acknowledge issues, and list them clearly. Don't minimise their importance from an adult perspective.
- Discuss issues in depth. Don't offer generic advice or platitudes. Include parents and/or teachers where it is appropriate to do so; but allow the young person to keep control as far as possible.

- Plan carefully. Agree a realistic course of action, and a timescale for reviews. Be creative and innovative. Think of what might work in a best-case scenario, then work towards that goal.
- Agree who should be told or given sensitive information (often, pupils would agree to individual staff being given more information but as a support strategy, as with medical information – not for teachers to then discuss with the pupil on a one-to-one basis).
- Monitor progress, or lack of it. Be prepared to tear up a plan and write another one.
- Evaluate. Get honest, written feedback from everyone concerned. It is useful to do this in order to acknowledge in a balanced and measured way what worked, and what didn't.

Chapter 4: Provisions and collaborations

Alternative Education Base activities

The aim of the Alternative Education Base was always to return pupils to mainstream lessons as soon as reasonably possible, and with that in mind pupils who could not remain in their class for whatever reason continued as far as was practical with the same classwork within the Base. This was negotiated with individual teachers, with parental involvement. Pupils with medical problems were also allowed to use the Base at lunchtimes and other intervals. Friends of these pupils could have their lunch with them in the Base, but entry was by a strict 'Pass System' supervised by an on-duty member of Base staff.

> *Key Point*
>
> *The aim of the Alternative Education Base was always to return pupils to mainstream lessons as soon as reasonably possible.*

In addition to helping pupils on an individual basis, the Base also offered some routine activities – for example, an induction programme for all new pupils who joined during the course of the school year. A three- to five-day 'easing in' period allowed these new pupils to settle in quickly, but also to have intensive support while they were trying to find their way around or meeting new staff and their peer group. 'Buddies' would take new pupils around and introduce them to people at breaks and lunchtimes. Staff from the Base also worked with EAL (English as an Additional Language) staff to support pupils from abroad, and made use of bilingual students to act as helpful go-betweens when new pupils whose first language was not English were unsure of anything.

A Reduced Timetable Group was provided for pupils aged around 14-16 identified as likely to benefit from social skills support. This was an in-house programme incorporating groupwork, a health and fitness programme, first aid, money management and a food preparation and cookery course. The Classroom Assistant/Art Specialist developed and delivered creative elements of the programme such as clay work, jewellery-making, painting and framing. Work with older pupils was weighted towards preparing for work, college or training. Each year, two final year pupils were assigned to work with the Base teacher to help deliver the Reduced Timetable programme, and senior pupils in the school more generally were recruited to offer peer support to younger pupils in the Base.

For pupils struggling with specific issues, one-to-one work with staff such as the school Youth Worker and the Youth Strategy Social Worker was arranged. One-to-one sessions also took place with a Base teacher qualified in anger management; this was for pupils who had a history of confrontation, and who were therefore in danger of exclusion or permanent exclusion. Groupwork was also organised targeting particular year groups and problem areas – for example, a first-year transition group for vulnerable pupils new to the school, social and health issues groups, and summer holiday groups.

Finally, activity was not limited to supporting pupils within the school. Contact was maintained with a number of young people who had left school but still needed ongoing support, often emotional or relating to career choice. Base staff also sometimes supported other members of teaching staff who were having difficulties with personal, emotional or health problems. There is typically little space in schools for staff to get immediate confidential support, and stresses can often go unnoticed. In the Base, staff could find a sympathetic ear, a quiet space and respite in what can be a relentless environment.

Hosting of pupils from other schools

The Base school worked with five other schools in the same city to offer a practical solution to the problem of pupils who were seriously underachieving in their 'home school', and thus in danger of permanent exclusion. The project involved developing support strategies for pupils, who were hosted for an agreed period (between eight and sixteen weeks), to one of the five other schools. This was run as a collaborative project for three years and was then embedded into the schools' practice and provision. Joyce was the In-School Coordinator for this project, and after negotiation with the other School Coordinators, she drafted guidelines for this provision which were later adopted by the City's Department for Education:

- To be a non-punitive solution for pupils at risk of temporary or permanent exclusion from school.
- To be pupil-centred, and to give pupils an opportunity to experience success and develop resilience.
- To challenge negative behaviours and to negotiate a realistic plan of action in a positive environment.

- To honestly address home school issues – often around peer status, behaviour and attainment.
- To give pupils a fresh start in a new environment – with support from the host School Coordinator.
- To maintain, as far as possible, course choice subjects (with damage limitation as the guide – better to reduce subject choice than to face further or permanent exclusion from school).
- To provide good support and communication to staff, parents and the home school.
- To use an eight-week review to decide whether to extend the period of hosting for another eight weeks, to enrol the pupil in the new school, or to return the pupil to his or her home school.

Hosting was a labour-intensive provision, but one that cost very little for schools to manage, and it was a great success for many pupils who were previously stuck in a cycle of underachievement. The fact that all schools in the group were still hosting for each other many years later was a testament to the trust and commitment that was built up, and the value that all who were involved placed on this as an effective intervention for pupils who needed to re-engage with education.

The foundation of success

The Alternative Education Department was an exemplar of best practice in pastoral care in education. In providing refuge, support and encouragement to young people of secondary school age who might otherwise have entered downward spirals, it changed many lives for the better. Its key lesson is that every individual and situation is unique – there are no easy, 'catch all' answers when it comes to resolving the difficulties that young people may experience at school.

> **Key Point**
>
> *Every individual and situation is unique – there are no easy answers when it comes to resolving the difficulties that young people may experience at school.*

We do know, however, that the sooner problems of this kind are faced and addressed, the greater the likelihood of young people building resilience and being able to cope as adults. Serious problems seldom just go away by themselves, and issues that are not acknowledged or properly managed can lead to a raft of problems including mental health difficulties in later years. Resources invested in preventative work in childhood and adolescence is always money well spent. It can help to address important mental health problems at a point where they are more easily managed than in adulthood.

The guiding approach of this book, therefore, is that supporting children and young people who are struggling with teenage school difficulties means tailoring help to the individual. For teachers and schools, the approach taken must be pupil-centred, flexible, and adapted to needs and personality. For parents and carers, whose greatest fear may be an intervention that removes a child from their care, it is important to have faith in authority and to have confidence in disclosing and discussing problems. Positive relationships and mutual trust are always the surest foundation for success.

Ten key things to know about teenage school difficulties

1. *Nearly every pupil* is at some point likely to experience difficulties in the secondary school years.

2. Teenage school difficulties are not restricted to the pupil's academic work.

3. Teenage school difficulties extend beyond the environment of the secondary school.

4. Approaches to teenage school difficulties must be non-punitive where possible, and when punishment around behaviour is appropriate as part of the school discipline policy, it should be matched with a collaborative, restorative approach.

5. Teenage school difficulties can fall under general categories, but they affect every pupil differently, so the approaches to support must be tailored to the individual pupil.

6. Young people must be kept at the centre of dialogue and the planning of support.

7. All support has to be planned and provided in the context of child support, other statutory guidance and other professional agencies.

8. Good provision is based on establishing open and trusting relationships with parents and carers as part of the whole-school ethos, and this should underpin the pastoral system.

9. Good provision has to be a school-wide priority and fully supported at management level, with appropriate staff training and development to provide a holistic approach.

10. Good provision will require links and well-developed liaison with the local community and all other relevant agencies.

Part 2: Primary school and transition issues

Chapter 5: Primary school

When a child is enrolled in primary school, things change for him or her in terms of additional influential adults in their lives, and the structure of their day – which might involve more discipline, greater routine, access to wider friendship groups and experiences of having to cope without

> *Key Point*
>
> Early intervention is always the key to offering effective support to a child and his or her family.

the supervision of their usual care giver. Much can be learned from watching reception stage children interacting with other children in a play setting, and the importance of good training for staff in recognising and addressing concerns at an early stage cannot be underestimated.

Primary schools as an environment for children are very different to secondary schools. They are usually smaller, and have fewer pupils on the school roll. Children encounter fewer staff and other children during the day. They are supervised more in a classroom setting than at secondary school, and are often in age-restricted play areas, so that reception will not mix socially with older children. A primary class typically spends most of its day as a unit, with one member of staff (although there may be classroom assistants and other specialists who teach the class at set times during the week), so the relationship with the class teacher is crucial. Relationships between the child, teacher and home must be nurtured and well managed.

Early intervention is always the key to offering effective support to a child and his or her family, and to making a difference at what is a crucial time in a young person's development, but it must be a two-way process between school and home. Parents should ensure that the school is aware of any additional support needs that their child may have, and keep the school informed of any change of circumstances that is likely to affect the child's health, wellbeing or welfare. Separation, divorce, financial problems, bereavement and other issues that are painful for adults are also difficult for children to absorb and deal with, and can manifest in changes in behaviours and attainment at school. This can have long term consequences for the child. For more information on such issues see Chapters 27-29.

Although primary aged children may be less inhibited than secondary school pupils when talking about their home and family life, those in difficulty do not always have the vocabulary or emotional maturity to identify the cause of their distress with a view to seeking support. Trained primary school staff will be alert and sensitive to subtle, as well as more obvious, signs that something is wrong, and can therefore investigate possible causes for changes in behaviour, mood, attendance or general wellbeing, as part of the ongoing pastoral support of pupils in their care. Make sure that all staff have the opportunity for discussion of and reflection on their professional training. There should be a good supervision system in place for staff to bring concerns about children in their care. This will allow them to feel supported as a matter of course in their professional life, and not just at flashpoints.

Parents should work in collaboration with school staff to support their child. Intervention should not be seen as a punishment or a criticism of parenting skills, but as a long-term benefit for the child. If outside agency support is suggested, parents can ask for an inter-agency meeting to agree issues and approaches, and to see what might be done to support this work.

How to help – supporting your child at primary school

 Read all school documentation, and mark anything you need to know about. Attend any pre-school visits that are offered, and take another trusted adult with you if you are uncomfortable. It is useful to see classrooms and the school environment, and to meet some of the staff before your child starts to attend the school. Ask lots of questions!

 Identify any problems you might see for your child at the school, and ask about them. If you know that your child will need additional support, make sure the school is aware of this and ask to meet all relevant staff who may become involved in your child's care. This might include auxiliary and medical staff as well as teaching staff.

 Have a one-to-one meeting with your child's class teacher, and establish a good relationship. This helps to defuse potentially difficult situations, and it is always good to put a name to a face. This teacher will be a key person in your child's life, so it is important that you can communicate with him or her in a climate of trust and cooperation.

Keep up to date with the school website regarding term dates, holiday dates and school events – particularly in the later primary years leading to transfer to secondary school, where the process of being new in a new environment starts again and all the pre-primary school advice should be revisited in order to aid a smooth transition. For specific information on transition to secondary school, see Chapter 7.

The transition to secondary school

When the time comes for a child to move up from primary to secondary school, careful management is required. The structure of the school day and week is very different in secondary school, and this can be challenging for any pupil; however, it may be particularly problematic for pupils with additional support needs or who find change stressful. So keep in mind that while many young people are excited about the move to secondary school, for others – especially those with complex needs – it can be terrifying.

When children reach secondary school age, they are often more aware of their situation than they were during their primary school years, and more able to identify and articulate issues that are problematic. They may be less reliant on or attached to their parents, and less willing to disclose personal information to staff. They should all be aware of Child Protection Guidelines, or the equivalent, by this stage, and aware of who they can approach for support in and out of school. This might include youth workers, support staff and extended family members or other parents in the community.

Good transition work between primary and secondary school is vital. Personal Pupil Records or the equivalent should include all relevant information for secondary school pastoral care staff to allow them to offer the required level of support from the outset. Early intervention and/or the continuation of support for young people is invaluable to allow pupils to settle in what is a completely new and often intimidating environment. For more information on the transition to secondary school, see Chapter 7.

How to help – how schools can support children and families

☞ Invite parents and carers to an induction meeting in school, and welcome them in a non-threatening environment. Show them around and introduce them to staff. It is good for parents to get to meet all support and auxiliary staff as well as teachers, because parents are the first point of contact if there is cause for concern. They should meet their child's class teacher(s) at the earliest opportunity and foster a good, positive relationship. Face-to-face meetings at this stage can defuse situations that arise later, and take the heat out of potential conflict.

☞ Issue all parents with a School Handbook that gives basic information in a palatable form that is not threatening or intimidating – otherwise, it will not be read by many people (this is a problem that schools often have in producing documents and letters to parents). Invite questions about procedures, classroom management and discipline to avoid confusion, and explain clearly what school policies are on these issues.

☞ Have a clear, easy-to-follow website with essential information – school times, dress code, term dates, contact numbers and so on. Make sure it is updated regularly, and use it as a vehicle to celebrate class activities and achievements. Keep the tone friendly, and always invite parental feedback and involvement in the school's activities. Invite parents to join in with some of these activities, and don't allow this to be seen as the domain of just a few parents such as those on the School Board; many parents don't feel comfortable on committees, but are willing and able to offer other skills or simply their time.

☞ Inter-agency work is crucial. Schools should investigate all outside agencies that are or can be involved in the working life of the school, and keep looking for new resources. There is often someone on the staff who is especially skilled at getting access to new people, resources and funding. Giving that person the freedom and flexibility to visit and complete funding applications will be time well spent!

☞ Address concerns about a child as soon as possible. Be aware of family circumstances, and always start with a positive approach. Also, be aware that emotions can be high from the outset. A calm approach and a non-threatening, non-judgemental manner is always the best way forward. Keep parents informed of any other agencies who might become involved with their child – do not present this as a fait accompli, but as a widening of expertise to support everyone.

☞ Keep accurate, detailed records of any meeting with parents and other professionals, with a solution-focused approach. Be aware that there are some cases where there will have to be long-term support for the child or family, beyond primary school age, so it is vital that all records of meetings and strategies employed to date are available for the secondary school to take forward, or build on.

☞ For pupils with support needs of any kind, primary to secondary school liaison is crucial. There should be clear, pre-transfer meetings with key staff from the secondary school, and the chance for parents to be involved in this process as early as possible, before the child is faced with such a significant change. Investigate the possibility of group work to support vulnerable people during primary to secondary transition, using primary and secondary staff. This work could take place over the summer break to ease young people into their new environment, and should continue, if possible, during the first term of secondary school.

Chapter 6: Teenage transitions

Being a teenager and coping with all that comes with the territory is a painful time for many young people. It is a time of huge change, often involving a new school, new demands, increases in expectations, negotiating peer relationships and huge physical and hormonal changes. For parents, it can be like walking a tightrope while blindfolded. They sometimes mourn their apparent loss of position as a person of importance in their child's life.

Key Point

Many 'difficult' pupils are the ones who have had, or are having, difficulties, and they need support to make sense of their world.

Young people often judge their lives against what they see of their peers, and can easily feel marginalised and isolated by social, family and emotional problems that change the playing field for them at what is a crucial time in their development. Many 'difficult' pupils are the ones who have had, or are having, difficulties, and they need support to make sense of their world. In addition to exam pressure, relationship issues, family problems and the leap into the unknown from adolescence to adulthood, they are subject to additional pressures and concerns stemming from the wider social, economic and political climate:

- Employment prospects in a collapsing world economy
- Access to Further/Higher Education, and student debt
- Affordability of housing – being able to live independently of parents
- Concerns for the planet and sustainability for future generations

Common changes in the early to mid-teenage years

The following changes are often seen in pupils during the first few years at secondary school:
- They no longer spend so much time with their parents or carers.
- They no longer see their parents or carers as always (or ever!) being right.
- They can be challenging in their attitude to what would be normal family discipline and rules.

- They question authority in the home and at school.
- They attach more to their peers.
- They become more independent, or seek more independence.
- They seek more privacy.
- They can become reluctant to respond to questions about school, friends and activities.
- They can seem anti-social and alienated from their own family, but be described as polite and outgoing by friends' parents, and by teachers.

All of the above are things that most parents of teenagers will identify with, but sometimes young people begin to exhibit evidence of not coping, and this is what concerns us here. When a young person experiences problems, the people most likely to notice that something is wrong are those who regularly spend time with them: parents, carers, family members, teachers and friends. They will often be able to identify specific concerns and/or changes in behaviours that are indicative of a need for some sort of intervention.

Teenage concerns commonly identified by parents, carers and family members

While some things that can initially appear problematic are just part of the normal journey through the teenage years, parents and carers often know when there is more to the story. In such instances, early liaison with a pastoral care teacher is crucial. It would be hoped that parents and carers would already know which member of pastoral care staff to approach. It is important to list the concerns, to give as much information as possible, and for a meeting to take place to look at the full picture from the school's perspective and knowledge of the pupil. If this is a pupil who is new to the secondary school setting then it is important to gain the pupil's trust, and for any intervention to be perceived by the pupil as supportive, not punitive or as the school and/or parents 'ganging up' against him or her.

How to help – warning signs of distress for parents and carers

☞ Changes in mood and/or mood swings, including aggression, depression, anxiety, tears and tantrums.

☞ Changes in sleeping habits – not sleeping, disrupted nights, nightmares, bed-wetting, reluctance to get out of bed in the morning.

☞ Changes in eating habits – overeating, refusing to eat with others, hiding food, controlling food.

☞ Change in personal hygiene habits – lack of interest in personal care or appearance.

☞ Apparent disregard for the feelings of others – a seeming inability or refusal to acknowledge issues, the impact of their behaviour, and to engage in any meaningful discussion.

☞ Lack of interest in school subjects, failure to meet deadlines, anxiety about a subject, teacher, class or particular day of the week.

☞ Feeling unwell more often than usual – for example upset stomach, headaches, illness on a Sunday evening or before school in the mornings, feigned illness.

☞ Increased absenteeism compared to previous attendance, refusal to attend school, truancy for part or full days.

☞ Reluctance to leave the house to be with friends – disengagement, withdrawal from usual social activities, hobbies and interests.

Teenage concerns commonly identified by teachers and schools

As teachers see pupils for only a few hours per week, it can take several weeks for changes to be noticed or monitored. Behaviour changes are most likely to be the ones to be flagged up across the board. When several staff report concerns about the same pupil, the pastoral care or Guidance teacher would usually circulate a request for an update from all subject teachers. This can lead to an interview with the pupil, then with parents. At this stage, the home situation can sometimes be revealed as also causing concern. Again, a non-punitive approach at this stage is the one that is likely to achieve the best outcomes – although normal school discipline procedures would usually have to be followed initially.

> ## How to help – warning signs of distress for teachers and schools
>
> ☞ Poor attendance.
>
> ☞ Failure to complete work, meet deadlines or hand in homework.
>
> ☞ A change in attainment or in apparent interest; disengagement in the classroom.
>
> ☞ A change in behaviour – poor or challenging behaviour which is not consistent with previous character.
>
> ☞ Concerns around interactions with other pupils and/or significant changes in friendship groups.

Teenage concerns commonly identified by friends

School friends are less likely to go directly to a pastoral care teacher, or the young person's parents or carers, but they can provide very useful information from another young person's perspective about what seems to be going on. It is a huge burden for a young person to carry anxiety for another young person's wellbeing, but there is often a natural reluctance to betray a confidence and any intervention by staff must therefore be handled very carefully. The intervention must be seen to be supportive of the young person, and should strive to maintain the friendship at all costs.

Clear discussion of the Child Protection Guidelines (or equivalent) should already have taken place with all pupils at the start of their school journey, so this is often a good way to start this delicate conversation – as a supportive approach to protect someone's health and wellbeing. If a young person approaches a member of staff about his or her concern for a friend, this should be acted on quickly and sensitively. Support should be given to both pupils, to maintain the friendship and to deal with any issues raised.

How to help – warning signs of distress for friends

☞ Conflict with friends and changes in friendships.

☞ Changes in socialising inside and outside school.

☞ Dropping out of team activities, including sports and youth clubs.

☞ Confiding worrying thoughts – expressing anxiety to friends, or to one friend in particular.

☞ Apparent difficulties relating to the young person's health, mental health and/or welfare.

Chapter 7: Transitioning to secondary school

The transition from primary to secondary school is a time of major change for pupils, presenting them with a range of different challenges including the structure of the school day, the increased number of teachers they interact with each week, new subjects, more homework and the possible disruption of friendship groups. Some children can find this new environment exciting, and they look forward to the change. Other children, however, having been the big fish in the small pond of their primary school, will dislike suddenly being the small fish in what will undoubtedly be a much bigger pond. Chapter 17 includes information on how transition can be managed to help pupils with specific difficulty in this area.

> *Key Point*
>
> *The transition from primary to secondary school is a time of major change for pupils, presenting them with a range of different challenges.*

How parents and carers can facilitate school transition

Parents and carers can help with the transition from primary to secondary school by making an effort to get to know everyone involved with the support of their child, and keeping everyone informed of any known or likely issues. Participate in induction activities, and be prepared for your child to hear scary stories that have become urban myths about things that happen to pupils as part of their induction. Reassure them that every new intake hears the same stories, and passes them on in turn. If your child has a sibling at the school, this can be helpful; however, do not expect the sibling to be able to look out for your younger child in school, or to spend their breaks or lunchtimes with them. This is not manageable, it places an unfair burden of responsibility on the older child, and it could prevent the younger child from integrating with his or her peers as a critical point in their social development.

Your child is likely to be anxious before the start of their first term at secondary school. While this is normal, do not dismiss his or her anxiety. Go over everything, and be well prepared for the first day – with uniform ready, school bag packed, lunch arrangements made, and travel plans sorted so that there are no early morning panics. Expect your son or daughter to be very tired after school, and to need more sleep at weekends. He or she will be dealing with new people, new subjects, many more teachers and almost certainly an increase in the volume and variety of homework. Add in all the physical changes that take place around this age, and it is only natural for this to have an impact at home.

How to help – a parent's guide to secondary school transition

☞ Use your existing relationships with primary school teaching and support staff to alert them about any concerns you have about the move to secondary school and its likely impact on your child.

☞ Most schools offer induction meetings where you can see the school and meet key staff. Attend and make yourself known to those who will be directly involved with the teaching and pastoral care of your child.

☞ Ask if there is an induction visit for pupils and, if so, what it involves. Go over the format of this visit with your child several times, listening to any concerns and trying to address them. If you don't have the answers then ask the school for clarification – or ask your child's primary teacher to do this, and to work with you to offer reassurance.

☞ If your child has an older sibling already at the school then engage his or her support in helping to make your younger child less anxious – but do not ask the older child to interfere or provide company during the school day. Many friendship groups are formed in the first couple of weeks of school, and are difficult to break into once established.

☞ Ask if there is a 'buddying' system in the school. In the Base school, two or three sixth form pupils were attached to each new intake class. They took pupils to classes during the three-day induction visit, and kept in contact with the same class when they started school – making themselves available at breaks and lunchtimes to encourage pupils to ask for help more readily than they might ask staff.

Be prepared for your child to be anxious before the start of the first term in secondary school. This is normal. Try to stay calm, be matter of fact, and don't allow your own anxiety to transfer to your child. Have plans made and everything ready ahead of time. If possible, arrange for your child to travel to school with another new intake pupil. Expect the early days to be tiring, and plan something nice for the end of the week or the weekend so your child can focus on that.

How teachers and schools can facilitate school transition

Schools can assist with the transition process for their new intake of pupils by establishing strong links with all feeder schools in the area, and starting the transition process early for children in their last year of primary education. This might involve visits to the primary schools in order to speak to classes, discuss life in secondary school and see these pupils in an established, comfortable setting with their peers and a teacher who knows them well. If possible, some secondary teaching staff could teach alongside the primary school class teachers, to assess work covered and to introduce different work methods. This is labour-intensive, so it is likely that only one or two subject departments will be able to staff and manage it.

How to help – transition tactics for teachers and schools

 When visiting primary schools, ask the class teachers for advice about pupils who may struggle with the transition, and who are likely to need extra support. Ask about pupils who should be separated from each other and those who would benefit from being kept with another pupil. This information is invaluable for staff making up class lists, mixing pupils from the feeder primary schools.

 Invite parents and new intake pupils to an information evening in the secondary school. This is not like a traditional parents' evening, but one where people are able to look around the school and ask general questions. Parents should be made aware of who the pastoral care (or Guidance) staff are, and what support they can offer pupils.

Organise an induction visit for new intake pupils. This might take the form of a two- or three-day visit, where pupils will spend time in the school, go to classes, and get a feel for the place before they leave primary school for the summer holidays.

 Use senior pupils to 'buddy' new pupils for the induction visit, and for the first week or so of the new term. If additional funding is available, youth workers could be employed to do summer holiday transition work with pupils identified by feeder primary schools as vulnerable.

Secondary transition case study 1: Megan and Ella

Megan and Ella had been in the same primary school class since they were five years old. They were anxious about their move to secondary school because they didn't want to be separated. Their parents approached the primary school class teacher who agreed, based on her knowledge of the girls, that it would be detrimental to their welfare for them to be separated. This was discussed with the secondary school Guidance Team Leader during transition discussions. The girls went into the same classes, although they were separated for practical subjects due to the alphabetical split of the group for smaller-size sets. Megan and Ella coped well with the move to secondary school. By the time they were in their second year, and beginning to think about subject choices, they were still friends but more confident of their places in the wider peer group, and were able to move independently into the next phase of their schooling.

Secondary transition case study 2: Cameron and Jake

Cameron and Jake were close friends, and a powerful force in their primary school class. They were both pleasant pupils, but could be disruptive, or intimidate others in class. They had a series of low-level reports for disruption and/or discipline issues in their school files, and they were often separated in group activities to minimise the risk of negative behaviour. They were keen to be kept together at secondary school, but their parents and class teacher agreed that this would not be in their own or the school's best interests. This information was fed into the transition arrangements, and the boys were placed in different secondary school classes. They both managed well, quickly formed new friendships, and achieved better results when apart. They remained friends throughout their school years, and were members of the same sports club. They became sociable, confident young men who both benefitted from this early decision to separate them.

Chapter 8: Organisation

The increased number of subjects studied in a broad secondary school curriculum, each with at least one teacher, increases the need for pupils to be organised, to take more responsibility for homework and to meet deadlines. This extra work pressure can be very challenging for some pupils. Many very able and motivated pupils can come unstuck because they have not developed the skills of planning, prioritising and structuring their commitments, and this can have a serious impact on their academic success. Support in developing these skills will not only benefit the child in the classroom; it will also be of great value outside of school, and beyond school.

> *Key Point*
>
> *Many able and motivated pupils come unstuck because they have not developed the skills of planning, prioritising and structuring commitments.*

Teachers and schools can encourage good organisation among pupils by having a clear homework policy, and by providing pupils with homework planners that are checked and signed by parents and staff. Subject departments should be encouraged to publish submission dates for larger pieces of work on the school website, and reminder dates should be included in any newsletters issued to parents (usually on a term or quarterly basis). Include organisational and study skills in the social education programme (PSHE or equivalent), and listen to pupils' views about the amount of homework they are getting. If there seems to be an issue around too many subjects giving homework at the same time, then this should be raised with subject leaders. Pastoral care staff should always work with teaching staff on a one-to-one basis if they become aware of personal or family issues that are affecting a young person's ability to complete homework or to meet deadlines.

Parents and carers should try to discuss with their children the work they are doing. Show an interest but don't interfere, and avoid trying to re-teach things differently to the way they are being taught in class as this can lead to confusion. If your child has a learning difficulty, it may well be that he or she does need different teaching methods and this can be discussed and carried out in collaboration with the school. Pupils across the entire range of abilities can be affected by difficulties with processing speed or working memory, so don't assume that because your child is 'bright' he or she cannot be struggling with the demands of extra workload and responsibility.

How to help – assisting with organisation

☞ Check homework planners regularly – your child may not be the most reliable source of information about homework that has been set!

☞ Make sure there is a quiet space in the house where your child can work uninterrupted, and where there are not too many distractions.

☞ Make an agreement about when homework should be done. A routine is good. For younger pupils, it is often best done once they've had a snack or brief rest after getting home from school, either before or after their evening meal. Don't allow your child to do homework after an evening spent watching TV, or in the morning while having breakfast and getting ready for school.

☞ Don't turn a conversation about schoolwork into a lecture, or a row. If homework is taking far longer than intended, it is worth exploring the possibility that your child might have additional learning needs.

☞ If you have concerns about the amount of homework and deadlines, investigate this in a calm way. The school may have a homework policy, and individual subject departments may publish submission dates at the start of the session.

Organisation case study 1: Tom

Tom's teachers became concerned that he was failing to meet homework deadlines and coming up with a variety of unacceptable reasons for this. He was reported to his Guidance Teacher for failure to get his homework planner checked and signed, and so was called in for a chat. He was initially reluctant to discuss this but, when it was suggested that his parents be informed, he became upset. He disclosed that his father was unwell and was behaving erratically, so Tom was not able to concentrate or complete work on time. His punctuality had also become an issue, and this was because he was trying to help his mum to get his father dressed and organised in the morning. Tom was unsure what was wrong with his father, but knew from overheard conversations between his mother and his grandmother that it was something serious. The Guidance Teacher contacted Tom's mother, and learned that Tom's father had just been diagnosed – in his forties – with early onset Alzheimer's disease, and the prognosis was not good.

In order to support Tom, the Guidance Teacher got permission to tell staff that there were extenuating family circumstances, and that he should be given leeway for any deadlines – that he would be unlikely to complete work at short notice, but would make efforts to catch up. He was given free access to the Alternative Education Base and school library for quiet study time, as he could not get this at home. His father was hospitalised within six months, and although this alleviated the daily chaos in the home, it created other problems for Tom and his family that required intensive support, involving liaison with outside health support agencies, for the remainder of his school career. Tom was discussed at the Pupil Support Group where it was agreed he would be given a 'self-referral' card for the Base and that he would be referred for one-to-one Youth Worker support in school to negotiate any further issues for him as they arose.

Organisation case study 2: Scarlett

Scarlett settled in quickly to secondary school and enjoyed the wider range of academic subjects and social/extra-curricular activities on offer. She coped well with the initial transition, but missed some school during the Spring term due to glandular fever and became noticeably anxious about her return. Although she had completed most of the classwork, she had missed out on social interaction and the general life of the school. Her parents felt that she was becoming depressed at home, and were keen to engage help to help her return, but they also acknowledged that it would be some time before she was physically and emotionally back to full strength.

A meeting was set up in school with Scarlett, her parents, her Guidance Teacher, the Alternative Education Base Teacher and the school Medical Auxiliary. Her Guidance Teacher had requested reports from Scarlett's subject teachers to gauge her progress and to identify any areas of concern, so this was a good starting point. Scarlett was doing well – she had managed to keep pace with everything apart from Science, but it was felt that she could catch up on practical experiments on her return. This meeting focused Scarlett's mind not just on what she hadn't done, but on what she had managed to do despite her illness, and this was a positive step towards her feeling better about returning to school.

It was decided that Scarlett would initially return for mornings only for the first two weeks as she was suffering fatigue, but that she would build on that each week after discussion at home and with her Guidance Teacher and the Base Teacher. It was also agreed that she would not take part in PE classes until her stamina had increased, and that she would spend these periods in the Base, catching up on work missed – or on some sleep if she needed a rest. Scarlett was given a self-referral card for the Base to use at any time on her return, and offered the choice of spending breaks and lunchtimes in the Base or outside with her friends as and when she could cope. She could also access the school Medical room at any time in the school day to chat to the Medical Auxiliary if she had any concerns or needed to take any medication. Scarlett's teachers gave her leeway with deadlines and submission dates, and the Maths and Modern Language departments assigned their Student Teachers on placement in the school to work with Scarlett on a one-to-one basis in the Base to give her extra tuition, and to revise the term's work.

Scarlett's return to school was carefully managed and agreed, with her own and her parents' input at every stage. Her confidence returned when she saw how well she was doing, and felt that the pressure to complete work was being set at her own pace. She was back at school full time by the summer holidays, and was fully recovered for the start of her second year.

Part 3: Secondary school and educational issues

Chapter 9: Increased workload

From the time pupils move into the middle school years, there is increased pressure on them to meet assessment deadlines, and to prepare for exams. There is often a continual assessment element to subjects, where the final examination grade is dependent on the pupil's attainment over several tests and/or graded papers. This can reduce the extreme stress associated with a single, end of course exam, but it can also represent a more constant form of pressure. Many subjects have an external dissertation-type assessment (known in some countries as a folio) which can at times feel like an albatross around pupils' necks.

> ## Key Point
> *From the time pupils move into the middle school years, there is increased pressure on them to meet deadlines and prepare for exams.*

It is important for pupils to recognise that levels of work and commitments with increase, but that they need not be passive in the face of these challenges. They can develop skills and strategies that they can draw on – skills and strategies that will help them not just to manage but to thrive. These skills will, of course, also be of great value to them in other areas of life.

These new challenges can be particularly hard for young people who are also coping with personal, family or social problems. Parents and carers should therefore keep their son or daughter's pastoral care teacher informed as much as possible, so that in-school forms of support can be accessed. When it comes to university entry, positive discrimination systems exist. They will vary from place to place, but they can offer extra assistance to someone who has been disadvantaged by personal, family or social circumstances.

Some secondary school students choose to take part-time jobs. Although the extra money is tempting, pupils should be discouraged from working too many hours, or to accept requests from employers to pick up extra hours, as this often comes at a cost. Some older pupils end up working longer hours in part-time work than full-time employed adults. A secondary pupil working towards national exams has a huge workload from school; if he or she is also working too many hours for an employer, something must eventually give – and more often than not it will be academic attainment.

How to help – adapting to increased workload

☞ Be aware of the increased pressure on your child, and the greater number of assessments. The situation can be made worse if pupils ignore, forget or fail to meet deadlines, so check the school website for information regarding deadline and submission dates for each subject.

☞ Be sure to acknowledge any family or personal problems that your son or daughter may be coping with, and that may impact educational attainment, and keep the school informed as much as possible.

☞ Make sure there is a dedicated space for study in the house – with room to leave books and other work materials lying out. It's a messy process, and it can be difficult to live with. Ideally the space should not be in the family living room, or a room with lots of distractions.

☞ Be realistic. Do not expect your son or daughter to be able to study for hours at a time. Breaks are needed – often fuelled with drinks and snacks. If your child claims to have been shut away studying for five hours – that's unlikely! Check that he or she is not just appeasing you and watching Netflix or becoming distracted on social media.

Teachers and schools can help with the challenges of increased workload by ensuring that all subject departments publish deadline dates for submission of assignments, and by making these available to parents and pupils on the school website and in newsletters. Subject teachers should keep pastoral care staff informed of any concerns regarding progress or attainment, and discussions should take place with any pupils that are causing concern.

All pupils should learn about organisational skills and study planning in PHSE classes or their equivalent, and advice on stress management should also be provided. This could cover mindfulness and other relaxation techniques, as well as more specific help in dealing with exam nerves and anxiety. As exams approach, senior pupils should be given access to quiet study facilities and a structured programme of study skills and revision classes should take place.

Increased workload case study 1: Phoebe

Phoebe was a senior pupil working towards her final year exams. She had a conditional offer for a place at university to study Politics and Economics. Although she was working steadily in her classes, she was not meeting deadlines for assessments in school, and not producing her usual quantity of work. There was no doubting her ability, but her commitment had gone 'off the boil', and she was unlikely to meet the conditions for her university entrance. One teacher reported that she was missing too many Friday morning classes, and that when she was there she was tired and lethargic.

It transpired that Phoebe was working almost twenty hours per week in a local shopping centre – where the shops stayed open until 8pm most nights. She was then going out socialising with friends on payday (Thursday), so she was not fit for much on Friday mornings. An urgent meeting took place in the school with Phoebe and her father, and it was pointed out that she was unlikely to make the grades for university if she continued with her current level of part-time work. Her father had already expressed concerns about this, but he was unaware of how much it had already affected her schoolwork. He was also shocked to learn how many hours she was working. Phoebe agreed that her university place was more important, and reduced her working hours to just a Saturday. She managed to recover lost ground and got her place – but she had fallen into a trap that pulls many pupils down at a crucial time.

Increased workload case study 2: Zak

Zak was the second oldest child in a large family, and shared a bedroom with a younger brother who was still in primary school. The household was loving but chaotic, and there seemed to be few rules around tasks or routines. Zak's grandmother lived next door, and helped with day care arrangements and holiday periods. Zak's father was a shift worker and his mother an agency nurse, so the family had few opportunities to spend time together.

Zak was doing well academically, and his second-year reports had indicated that he could possibly consider university application. He chose to follow eight academic subjects (the norm for his age group within his national curriculum), and his workload increased rapidly throughout his third year, with regular assessments and homework assignments.

After a few months, Zak began to struggle to meet deadlines in several subjects, and towards the end of his third year there were concerns that he might not achieve the levels previously expected of him when he reached his national examinations. A request for detailed reports from staff showed up common concerns: Zak coped well in the classroom, but failed to submit homework assignments or do revision. He had done badly in some assessment tests, and he had reacted negatively when challenged about this by one of his teachers. His enthusiasm for school in general seemed to have dipped and his mood was reported by staff as low or truculent.

Zak's parents were asked to come into school to meet with his Guidance Teacher and Year Head, in order to go over the class teachers' reports and identify a way forward that avoided Zak having to drop down into lower sets for some of his subjects. Zak and his parents were shocked by how much he had already fallen behind, but the staff reports were detailed and clearly showed the discrepancy between his ability and his achievement. This was used as the focus for a discussion to support him, and to get him back on track.

The real issue for Zak seemed to be that he could not get a quiet space anywhere in his house for any length of time to do his work, and he felt he was always being distracted by his younger siblings and the general noise of a busy household. Sharing a room with his younger brother was becoming an increasing problem, and Zak felt that there was an increased expectation as he got older that he should help around the house when his parents were at work. He agreed that he needed to organise a more structured work plan, but felt that his parents needed to make some changes too.

It was agreed that some restructuring of accommodation in the house was possible, and Zak was given a bedroom to himself with a desk and space to set out his books and notes without risk of them being moved. Zak would complete his household tasks (earning him an allowance) when he first arrived home from school, but his evenings would be free after tea, when he would be expected to do his schoolwork. Zak's parents and his grandmother worked together on a weekly schedule to allow a degree of forward planning and organisation of childcare for Zak's younger siblings.

Zak agreed to keep a detailed homework diary, and worked with his Guidance Teacher to organise his study plan. Teaching staff provided him with individual revision sheets highlighting gaps in his learning and missed assignments, and he was given the chance to re-sit some tests once he had completed this revision. He was encouraged to use the school library for private study after school or on half days, and his grandmother agreed that he could use her house for revision as he approached his final examinations. Getting organised to this degree was new to Zak, but it was necessary for him to achieve his academic potential. He did well in his exams, and was much more positive and prepared for the even greater workload that lay ahead.

Chapter 10: Subject choice

At some point in their secondary schooling, every pupil will be required to make subject choices. This typically involves narrowing down the number of subjects studied from a wide range to only those that will be followed through to exams. The time when subject choice takes place will vary; whenever it happens, there can be pressure to achieve the grades needed for teachers to allow entry to a subject and there is often increased worry about moving into the next, and more serious, stage of schooling. If pupils are unhappy with their decisions at this stage, it can set up problems for self-confidence, behaviour and attainment, and can lead to disengagement for some.

> **Key Point**
>
> *Whenever subject choice happens, there can be pressure to achieve grades and increased worry about moving into the next stage of schooling.*

It is crucial that young people are actively involved and engaged in this activity. They need to be supported to make realistic decisions, based on their own interests and playing to their strengths. Parents often need to take a step back here, and make sure that they really listen to and focus on their child's perspective. They may need to help their child to interpret school and careers guidance. As is always the case when good communication is needed, it must be seen as an ongoing process requiring respect, mutual trust and time.

When seeking to help children understand this process and make informed choices, parents and carers should look at staff reports and also consider the pastoral care teacher's knowledge of their son or daughter's strengths and weaknesses from an educational perspective. Investigating possible career options that would require certain subjects in order to qualify for entry to higher education or employment is helpful; at the same, it is unreasonable to expect a child to have a clear career choice or plan. Many pupils do not know what they want to do as a career, even by the end of secondary school, and others change their minds completely, often several times!

How to help – advising on subject choice

☞ Read all the subject choice information given out by the school to pupils and parents. Often, there is a booklet explaining subject outlines and entry to study at different levels for national exams.

☞ Listen to your child's opinions about what he or she would like to do, and don't decide his or her future based on your own aspirations. At the same time, discourage choices made largely on the basis of favourite teachers or friendship groups – these can change!

☞ Help your son or daughter to make a realistic choice and take time to do this. Use Careers Service staff, employers, online searches and any other available sources to inform your decisions.

☞ As far as possible, keep options open – it is better to choose a wider curriculum than to narrow down future possibilities.

Teachers and schools can help with subject choice by starting the dialogue early and revisiting it often, perhaps in PHSE education classes or equivalent. Look at previous years' options so pupils can have a 'dummy run' and see the likelihood of being able to get all their first choices, and make it clear that there will be entry requirements in some subjects. Engage the services of careers staff to speak to groups and carry out one-to-one interviews.

It is important to liaise with parents and pupils to ensure that appropriate choices are made. This can be a sensitive subject for some pupils and parents, especially those who may have unrealistic ideas of career choice or likely academic achievement. Pastoral care staff should carry out a one-to-one interview with all pupils to discuss options and school reports, and to flag up any likely problems at an early stage.

Subject choice case study 1: Hannah

Hannah was a well-behaved, hard-working pupil who enjoyed school and had skills across different subject areas. When her class was discussing subject choice options, she was adamant that she was going to be a doctor and was set on choosing her subjects accordingly. Her predicted grades were not in line with university entry requirements to study Medicine, so a series of delicate discussions with her Guidance Teacher, the school Careers Officer and her parents was required to get her to look at other options.

Although initially Hannah was devastated, she started to investigate other possibilities – still involving a career in the medical field – and eventually she decided to explore physiotherapy. She chose the subjects needed for entry to this, managed to get some work experience within the physiotherapy department of a local hospital, and did end up choosing this as her career.

Subject choice case study 2: Ethan

Ethan struggled to make his subject choice decisions for his middle school years. He was a pleasant pupil who worked hard, but he did not feel confident making decisions that would determine his course of study for the next two years. He had some additional support needs, and had benefitted from Learning Assistant support in several classes during his early secondary years.

Ethan was anxious about making the wrong decisions, and his mother felt unable to assist him as he got upset whenever the subject was raised at home. The subject choice booklet and his recommended grades had been issued, his class was discussing choices in social education classes, and the deadline for making a final subject choices was looming.

A meeting was held in school with Ethan, Ethan's mother, the Head of Support for Learning, the Alternative Education Principal Teacher and the Guidance Teacher to help Ethan to feel more confident about his subject choices and about the transition to the next stage of his school career. It was agreed that Ethan would study a reduced number of subjects, and that he would join the Reduced Timetable Social Skills group offered by the Alternative Education department. He would continue to get some Learning Assistant support, and this would be reviewed regularly by the Support for Learning department.

With additional support from the Careers Officer attached to the school and his Guidance Teacher, who liaised with teaching staff and the Support departments, Ethan made realistic subject choices and was reassured that he could cope with the demands of the coming year and beyond. He was given additional support to cope with the national exams (extra time and a reader and scribe), help with making later subject choices, and careers advice regarding the options that were available to him beyond school.

Chapter 11: Disengagement

Assessing levels of disruption, disaffection or disengagement in schools is difficult, for several reasons. The effects can be hard to quantify and measure, and schools may have different levels of motivation to report these difficulties. In 2014 Terry Haydn discussed four studies conducted in England over the previous ten years[2], and found that there appeared to be large variations, both between different schools and within individual schools.

> ## Key Point
> *It only takes one or two persistent offenders to significantly affect the quality of teaching and learning that takes place in a classroom.*

Years of experience have taught us that a significant amount of school staff time is taken up with behaviour-related issues, and this accounts for a high proportion of referrals from teaching staff to the pastoral care and Senior Management teams. Problems range from low-level disruption to full-blown outbursts of verbal and physical abuse, with everything in between. All schools have systems to manage behaviour, and most have a punishment and reward element built in so that positive as well as negative behaviour is observed and commented on. It is important that good behaviour is not taken for granted, but instead recognised for the value it has.

Low-level disruption is the 'dripping tap' in a classroom and, while the phrase makes it sound like a mild irritant, it is incredibly disruptive to learning. In a class of twenty or thirty pupils, it only takes one or two persistent offenders to significantly affect the quality of teaching and learning that takes place in a classroom. This is not a new problem, and it can cost a great deal to manage it effectively. To bring about change, we must understand what lies behind the behaviour. There are many things that can affect adult mood and the way we interact with others. This is the same for young people, but many of them have not yet developed the skill and maturity to cope in a busy environment and to deal with the challenges that come with that.

---

2 Haydn, T. (2014), To what extent is behaviour a problem in English schools? Exploring the scale and prevalence of deficits in classroom climate. Rev Educ, 2: 31-64. doi:10.1002/rev3.3025

Common triggers for low-level disruption in a classroom include:

- boredom
- inability to cope with the work
- lack of motivation
- disrupted attendance/falling behind with work
- learning difficulties
- health issues
- peer pressure and/or the need to feel accepted
- dislike of a subject or teacher, or conflict with a teacher
- problems at home
- low self-esteem
- mental health issues

Many of these factors are discussed elsewhere in this book, and they can all lead to a young person behaving poorly in class and ending up in a cycle of punishments, detentions, avoidance, conflict and more low-level disruption. If we add in potential poor subject choice for older pupils, along with a lack of vocational training, work experience or part-time further education courses, it is easy to see why pupils become disaffected.

The complaint most frequently made by disengaged pupils is that school is not geared for them, and they would rather avoid it than be bored or get involved in disruptive behaviour. Unfortunately, when funding is an issue and schools are financially weakened, there is often nothing left in the budget to allow creative timetabling with a higher staff/pupil ratio to work with these young people, or to buy in other specialist training and staff for innovative projects. Many schools do succeed in designing and running effective courses for some disaffected and disengaged pupils, but their quality and sustainability will vary. There is a real need to overhaul thinking to provide appropriate, high-quality courses for a section of the school population who can otherwise easily drift into long-term unemployment, dependency on state welfare and, as a result, feelings of disengagement from society.

When seeking to promote engagement or address disengagement, parents and carers should always be aware that problems at home can impact a child's behaviour at school. If you feel that this may be a factor, discuss it with your child's pastoral care teacher. There is a common misconception that children simply 'bounce back' after traumatic events, and that this means they will be fine in the long run. Young people don't just 'bounce back'; even if they seem to 'bounce' differently to adults, they are just as affected by trauma and can be just as badly damaged. Many develop protective layers that hide unresolved issues, sometimes not far from the surface.

How to help – managing disengagement

☞ Be a parent first, rather than trying to be your child's best friend. Young people need guidance and direction, and being the one who will say "no" to them is an important part of a parent's role.

☞ Speak to your child. Sit down several times a week to eat, chat and listen to them talk about what's happening for them. Otherwise, conversations will tend to take place only when things go wrong.

☞ Check homework diaries (especially for younger teenagers, who may struggle with workload), and be aware of deadlines so that you can help your child to organise work or complete assignments on time.

☞ If your child is coming into conflict with other pupils or staff, discuss this calmly and look for solutions together. If your child is getting regular punishments, discuss it with him or her and ask to meet with the pastoral care teacher to get a cross-curricular picture.

☞ Find out the facts. If there is no doubt about your child's culpability, support the school in its normal discipline procedures. Accepting the consequences of poor behaviour helps to build resilience and maturity, and what may be seen as 'entertaining' behaviour within a family may be disruptive to teaching and learning in a classroom.

☞ Poor discipline in school is often mirrored in increasingly poor behaviour at home. Ask for help from other agencies, including your GP, or investigate community and/or parent groups.

Teachers and schools can minimise the risk of disengagement among pupils by having a clear discipline policy, making sure it is stated in the school handbook, and including it in PHSE classes or equivalent. Every teacher should also have a copy of his or her classroom discipline code displayed prominently on the wall, and should refer to it at the outset of sessions with each new class so that there is no room for ambiguity.

If disengagement or disaffection is a result of inappropriate subject choice or lack of opportunities for young people, look for creative solutions to re-engage them. Use all other agencies, community links, the Careers Service and local employers to investigate other activities to stand alongside reduced attendance at school. Examples from the Base school included arranging for senior-year pupils to run a tea dance in a local adults' day centre, and doing garden and DIY tasks for local pensioners. Many disaffected young people cope perfectly well outside school when they are engaged in something meaningful to them, and which gives them positive reinforcement. Most class teachers can recognise this in the pupils they see drifting in middle to senior years, and it is frustrating for everyone when these young people are constrained by poor choices for vocational opportunities that will prepare them for the next stage of their life, beyond their school years.

How to help – preventing disengagement in schools

- Have a clear referral system for punishments, so that if low-level incidents escalate, they can be tracked and monitored.

- Class teachers should inform pastoral care staff of formal punishments issued. This might be done using a centralised computer system, allowing pastoral care staff to see patterns developing across the school and early intervention to take place.

- Include a positive referral system in the discipline system, to recognise and reward good behaviour and individual achievement. This is an effective motivator for some pupils with behaviour issues, because it recognises small steps in the right direction.

- Introduce anger management in school. Helping pupils to understand and manage feelings of anger can prevent outbursts in class and reduce exclusions. Make staff aware of the programme – some may find it useful to inform their own management practice.

- Celebrate all success at school prize-giving services – not just academic and sporting achievement. Allow pupils to decide new award categories as part of a whole-school consultation process.

Disengagement case study 1: Aaron

Aaron had a history of low-level behaviour issues from late primary school. He was easily distracted, distracted others, and underachieved academically because of this. He was reluctant to accept normal classroom discipline and would provoke confrontation if even mildly rebuked by staff. He was, however, popular with his peers and did not seem unhappy in school. He managed reasonably well in his first and second years, but his reputation as a 'likeable rogue' shifted in his third year, by which time he was a persistent, disruptive influence in classes where there was pressure for pupils to work more independently or in groups.

Aaron was frequently issued punishments for low-level disruptive behaviour, but seldom completed them. Soon he began to be excluded from classes. Aaron's parents were supportive of the school, and concerned that he was in danger of further, formal exclusion. His father had struggled at school and was pessimistic about his son's ability to turn things around. His mother's family had a small business, and Aaron had been promised a job there, so it was felt that everyone was just treading water until he could leave school.

Matters came to a head after an aggressive outburst in a practical classroom, where Aaron punched another pupil and damaged an expensive piece of equipment. He was immediately formally excluded from school, with conditions for his return to be agreed at a multi-agency School Liaison Group meeting, which he would attend with his parents. The meeting used a pupil-centred and solution-focused approach to investigate strategies to allow Aaron to return to school. It identified the problems, but also the areas that were going well, and looked to build on these. A revised timetable was drawn up, additional supports were put in place and a contract was agreed and signed by Aaron and his parents. This was to be reviewed monthly with his Guidance Teacher and the Alternative Education Department.

Aaron was given one-to-one anger management support from a teacher in the Base. He would agree strategies to cope with his behaviour, discuss problem areas and set targets on a weekly basis. Any behaviour referrals from teachers would be sent directly to this teacher and discussed as a priority. Punishments, sanctions and rewards would also be dealt with in this way.

Aaron was given a self-referral card to the Base, but this was to be closely monitored. He would be expected to continue with the work of any class he came out of, and he was to keep a folder in the Base with additional work for other subjects. He was removed from his Modern Language class permanently as this was identified as a subject where he did not work well, was too far behind to catch up, and was unlikely to pass the national exam. This timetable block was spent in the Base, working on other subjects.

Aaron's contract held him more in check, and the one-to-one help gave him a focus for building his confidence and mood. He developed more positive relationships, and in his fourth year the Anger Management Teacher linked him up with a community-based group which provided vocational training for young people and was centred around building positive relationships, work and employability. Aaron's behaviour improved, he was motivated by his one-to-one support, and he managed to avoid further exclusion from school.

Disengagement case study 2: Fourth year girls

Disruptive pupils and their impact on the teaching and attainment of others was always a frequent topic of discussion in school meetings, but it was felt that a particular group of four fourth year girls, with others on the fringes, had begun to cause so much disruption that going beyond normal sanctions and punishments was required. The girls were ignoring or flouting school behaviour rules, and they were seriously undermining the progress of other pupils in their classes. They were a tight group and a powerful force in the playgrounds and corridors, and it was felt that they were gathering a cohort of younger, vulnerable pupils into their sphere – as well as affecting not only their classes but the atmosphere in the wider school community.

Everyone knew who the girls were. Many staff liked them and were able to manage them singly or in low numbers, but as a group they were seriously underachieving and not much concerned about it. They had amassed a significant number of detentions and exclusions, and two were in danger of permanent exclusion from school. They had had several interventions and other forms of support over the years, but a crisis point had been reached.

The Alternative Education Department submitted a proposal to offer support not only to these girls, but also to staff in the school. A detailed programme was organised and agreed at a special planning meeting, and the girls were approached individually and interviewed before they were invited to apply for the programme. This formal approach was carefully managed to set this initiative apart as something different for the girls – non-punitive, but with clear goals and expectations on both sides as to what its aims and objectives were. It was not a given that all the girls would be accepted into the group, and their application to be part of it was voluntary (although a degree of persuasion did go on behind the scenes before the interviews began).

The girls had to complete a basic tick-box form covering attainment, attitude to school, areas that concerned them and formal exclusions to date. They completed this with some Base staff help on a one-to-one basis, and in confidence. The girls then met with the Alternative Education Principal

Teacher, who would manage the group – so that she could discuss more details and 'sell' the benefits to each of them. The girls all knew the teacher running the group, and had positive relationships with her, which made this exercise much easier. The four girls were all keen to be part of the group, and the formal arrangements were agreed with a start date the following week – to allow for contact with parents/carers, and to interview two other girls for inclusion (partly because they would benefit from it, but also to avoid the initial four from identifying themselves as the 'bad girls').

The Programme arrangements were as follows:

- The group would meet twice per week – all of Tuesday afternoon, plus a two-hour session before the end of the school day on Friday.
- The sessions would involve group work, social and health education, behaviour management and completion of academic work.
- Emphasis would be placed on health and sexual health education, as several girls were involved in risk-taking behaviour in the community.
- Each girl would have individual extra timetabled periods in the Base each week to catch up on any work missed on Tuesdays and Fridays.
- The girls agreed and signed a contract regarding attendance at the group, behaviour in school and individual aims/targets.
- The girls would agree a reward excursion every four weeks if all targets were met by the whole group. This was a great motivator for improved behaviour in school, and it had an immediate impact.
- The girls were encouraged to spend breaks in the Base, to avoid getting caught up in negative behaviour and coming into conflict with staff and other pupils, and to separate them from younger, vulnerable pupils.
- A youth worker would work with the Base Teacher to manage the out of school activities, and to offer one-to-one support if required.

Every girl completed the programme, which ran for the rest of their fourth year, with improved attendance and a marked difference in their self-esteem and attitude to staff and school. There were still some concerns about their behaviour, but they became individually and collectively better at drawing back from the brink. When exam time came, they all met expectations.

Chapter 12: Truancy and absenteeism

Chronic truancy and absenteeism are problems in many schools, and a high proportion of pastoral care staff time can be taken up trying to unravel unexplained non-attendance. In 2006 Gaynor Atwood and Paul Croll found that truancy levels increased steadily through secondary education, and that patterns of truancy carried on to later years[3]. Unsurprisingly, truancy is associated with negative educational outcomes.

> ## Key Point
> *If poor attendance becomes the norm, the young person's place in the peer group becomes tenuous and his or her prospects are diminished.*

Absence from school can be for whole days without parents' knowledge, for part of a day or just from a particular class. Genuine medical absences are exempt from this concern but, for some pupils, a history of non-attendance or patchy attendance can be traced back to primary school. If poor attendance becomes the norm for a young person in the early school years, he or she is seriously disadvantaged by the time he or she gets to secondary school. The young person's place in the peer group becomes more tenuous, and his or her academic prospects are diminished. Schools should therefore be alert to the possibility that poor attendance in primary school will extend to secondary school, and arrange an early meeting to establish a good working relationship. There is a much better chance of open, honest dialogue if the first meeting is not fraught or confrontational.

Parents do not always support schools where truancy is concerned, and sometimes they themselves did not always attend school, so there can be no real incentive for the children to get up and out each day. Worryingly, some young people are actively discouraged from attending school because they are being used as babysitters and carers for younger siblings. There should be clear instructions in the school handbook and on the school website compelling parents to contact the school in the morning if their child will be absent. There should also be information about when absences will trigger further action from the school, and who will be involved.

---

3 Attwood, G. & Croll, P. (2006) Truancy in secondary school pupils: prevalence, trajectories and pupil perspectives, Research Papers in Education, 21:4, 467-484, DOI: 10.1080/02671520600942446

However, in most cases of truancy the parents or carers are just as concerned as the school. They often feel helpless, and worry about the damage being done to their child's education. A cycle can become established that is difficult to break: absence leads to falling behind with work, which leads to losing touch with friends, which leads to a reluctance to return to school, which leads to more absence. When a young person is locked into this cycle, it becomes a hard task for parents and/or schools to break the pattern and get them back on track.

If truancy is found to be due to other in-school problems, or is the result of family upset or trauma, there should be a pupil-centred meeting in school with the young person, the parents and any relevant others to look at what supports can be put in place and how they should be monitored. Attendance Sheets are a good short-term strategy, but no pupil should be permanently placed on an Attendance (or Conduct) Sheet. Disengagement with school can be improved by taking a flexible approach to what is possible in terms of timetable, potentially allowing the pupil to do well in the subjects they enjoy and to leave classes where they underachieve and undermine the education of others. If there is already social work or other agency involvement with the family, the school should arrange inter-agency contact or a meeting to agree common working strategies to support the young person.

In countries such as the UK, where parents have a statutory obligation to ensure that their children attend school, there is legislation to prosecute those who collude with truancy or unexplained absenteeism. In practice this is very much a last resort, and the primary focus is always on getting the young person back into education. Where parents are just as concerned as the school, and are anxious to get things back on track as quickly as possible, there must be good cooperation, open and honest dialogue, and shared responsibility to try to effect change if the initiative is to be successful in the long term. Young people should be part of this dialogue, which should include a clear statement of the problem, discussion of reasons for non-attendance, possible solutions and an agreed plan of action.

How to help – minimising truancy and absenteeism

☞ Be clear that you have a statutory obligation to ensure that your child attends school regularly, and that all absences are accounted for. If there has been poor attendance at primary school, be alert that this can quickly become a bigger problem at secondary school and, if possible, discuss it with staff during transition meetings.

☞ If truancy becomes a problem, act quickly to prevent a pattern developing. Listen to your child's concerns and ideas for what may help. There may be an issue with an individual, a subject or some other pressure that is making your child want to avoid school.

☞ Don't allow your child to stay off school when you know there is no medical reason. This can be the start of a damaging cycle, and lead to conflict at home. Remind your child of your obligations as a parent, and of the potential penalties you could face. Contact the school and set up a meeting to discuss any difficulties.

☞ If, after exhausting all other possibilities, you still think that your child is very unhappy at school, investigate a new school. It may be possible for your child to be hosted elsewhere for a trial period, although this will vary from place to place and will depend on the number of schools within reasonable travelling distance.

☞ If truancy is an issue later in the secondary years, discuss it with the pastoral care team and Careers Service, which has a remit to work with final destinations for this group. There may be options to replace some school time with college or work experience.

Absenteeism case study 1: Freya

Freya was a bright but disaffected girl in her exam year. She had a history of poor attendance since she started at secondary school, although she had regularly attended primary school. Her parents had alcohol dependency problems and, although she was materially cared for, she did not have anyone checking that she got up for school or challenging any absences. Her mother supplied her with absence notes, so it became easy for her to quietly drift away from her education. The more she was absent, the worse she did academically. By the end of her third year, she was attending less than 60% of the time and had missed important deadlines for several of her subjects.

Her mood was low, and she was often confrontational with staff if she was challenged about attendance or deadlines for classwork and assignments.

Attempts to engage Freya's parents foundered, but her school managed to get excellent one-to-one youth worker support for her. It was agreed at the start of her fourth year that Freya would reduce her subjects. She dropped two subjects that she seldom attended, and where there was no realistic chance that she could make up the time. She came to the Base during these classes, and caught up with work that she had missed for her other subjects. One department assigned a student teacher who was on teaching practice in the school to work with Freya for two hours per week, and this was a huge success. Freya engaged with the young woman and completed all her assignments. This motivated her to do even more work. She was able to see proof of her ability quickly, and was soon outperforming many of her peers.

One of the support Base staff who had previously been a careers officer worked with Freya to look at further education applications, and found her work experience in a local company for one afternoon per week. This gave Freya's self-confidence a huge boost, and made the rest of the school more relevant for her. Her home situation was unlikely to change, and her parents did not push her to succeed, but Freya did it for herself. Without this intervention she would have drifted out of school as soon as she was old enough to leave, her chances of employment would have been poor, and it is likely that there would have been some strain on her mental health. Instead, she took up a college place, received additional funding from a charity supporting young people, and worked part-time to pay the rent on a flat in the city – thus allowing her to leave home and live independently.

Absenteeism case study 2: Kyle

Kyle had attended school well in his first and second years, but it became evident in his third year that there was a problem. He had missed several Mondays in succession, and other periods of patchy attendance were showing up. Although he always brought in a note to cover his absence, his Guidance Teacher felt that there was a pattern developing, and that Kyle was in danger of falling behind his peers and underachieving. He and his younger brother lived with his grandmother and, although they had regular contact with their mother, a Court Order had decreed that the boys would remain in their grandmother's care for the foreseeable future following a Child Protection investigation into issues around neglect.

Kyle had been in an accident when he was ten years old and sustained a head injury. He had since suffered headaches, mood swings and anxiety attacks. He complained that the headaches were getting worse, and this was the reason for his increased absenteeism. He had some mild Specific Learning Difficulties, and he was known to the Support for Learning Department in school. They had monitored him in his first- and second-year classes but saw less of him in his third year, as he had seemed to be coping well.

Kyle's Guidance Teacher asked the Education Welfare Officer (EWO) to carry out a home visit, and the EWO met with Kyle and his grandmother. She noted that Kyle was playing on a computer when she arrived and that he seemed relaxed and well, although his grandmother confirmed that he had been upset and anxious earlier that day when she asked him to get ready for school. She also confirmed that Kyle did seem to be getting more headaches, but would not go to the doctor and did not have regular medication. Kyle's grandmother was keen to get him back to school but reluctant to put additional pressure on him. She did agree to attend a meeting in school to look for strategies to support Kyle, and to the EWO and Guidance Teacher contacting the family doctor for background information.

A solution-focused meeting was set up in school and, although Kyle refused to attend, his grandmother came. She brought along a friend for support – someone who had also known Kyle since he was a baby and had a positive relationship with him. Kyle's pattern of absence was highlighted. His grandmother was shocked to see the extent of the problem on paper, and she agreed that there was an issue of anxiety around Mondays in particular. Kyle's Guidance Teacher had gathered reports from staff that detailed the concerns about the impact of these absences on his attainment.

It was agreed that the EWO would visit Kyle at home to go over the points raised at this meeting, and that she would bring him into school the next day to meet with his Guidance Teacher to discuss matters further, and for him to prepare a list of things that he wanted to address.

It was also agreed that Kyle's grandmother would make an appointment for him to see his doctor to investigate his headaches and anxiety. He would be given a self-referral card for the Base to use if he felt unwell, and he would spend the first two periods of each Monday in the Base to settle him and allow staff to assess his mood. The EWO would collect him each Monday for the next four weeks to re-establish a pattern of attendance. The Support for Learning Principal Teacher would meet with Kyle to gauge what supports could be put in place, and to ensure he was given additional support around exams. Kyle would meet weekly with his Guidance Teacher to agree and review attendance and attainment targets. He would also be referred for one-to-one and group work activities with the school-based youth worker.

Kyle's attendance improved immediately. His grandmother felt better supported to put pressure on him to attend school. She was reassured that there was no underlying serious medical condition after the family doctor's investigation, although he was diagnosed with stress-related migraine which was manageable with medication that he kept at home and which was also held in school for him by the School Nurse. His anxiety about his health and school lessened, and his self-confidence increased noticeably. He coped much better knowing that he had a supportive network of staff in school, and his headaches decreased. The School Nurse gave him good practical advice regarding relaxation techniques, and later encouraged him to use these as a coping strategy around exam preparation.

Chapter 13: School refusal

The terms 'school refusal' and 'school phobia' are often used interchangeably to describe the same problem, although there are differences between the two. While they can of course be associated with truancy and/or absenteeism, school refusal and school phobia should be understood as distinct issues, albeit equally difficult to solve. School refusal is, as the term suggests, a refusal – point blank, despite deals, negotiations, threats, promises and bribes – to go to school. School phobia is a genuine fear of going to school, and for young people in this situation the trauma they experience is physical and emotional, and distressing for their parents and others to witness. It can involve feelings of dread, nightmares, anxiety and panic attacks, sickness, mood swings, conflict, bargaining and self-harm.

> **Key Point**
>
> *While the terms 'school refusal' and 'school phobia' can be associated with truancy, they should be understood as distinct issues.*

Both situations result in the same thing – chronic attendance problems, and a lack of sustained education, with all the additional concerns that come with this. What is striking is how incredibly strong young people can be to resist so many adults trying to get them to do one thing. So although many of them might present as fragile, in some respects they can be exceptionally tough and powerful. They often have a sense of control at home and are unwilling to compromise or cooperate with any attempt to agree a plan to get them back into a pattern of attendance. Kearney and Bates (2005)[4] discuss the importance of early engagement of family members in helping to address the problem of school refusal/phobia.

If school refusal or school phobia is identified as a problem, action should be taken as soon as possible. The school should arrange a meeting between the child, parents and pastoral care staff to agree a plan. Let the young person lead so that goals are achievable from the outset. Engage the help of the Education Welfare Officer (EWO) or equivalent to meet with the family and go over their obligations for school attendance. The EWO can also suggest potential coping strategies, support parents whose child may be trying to undermine the plan at home, and encourage parents to contact their GP to further investigate possible causes and eliminate medical reasons for absences. Schools can

---

[4] Kearney, C. A. & Bates, M., Addressing School Refusal Behavior: Suggestions for Frontline Professionals, Children & Schools, Volume 27, Issue 4, October 2005, Pages 207–216, https://doi.org/10.1093/cs/27.4.207

also look at a modified timetable, a 'safe place' for parts of the school day and/or a phased return as options for moving forward – but under no circumstances should the young person be permitted to manipulate or backtrack on the agreement.

The plan should be reviewed, and new goals set. If there is no improvement after an agreed period, consideration can be given to the young person moving to another school – either on a hosting basis (where available) or permanently. If there is no likelihood of the young person being returned to mainstream education, then there should be an inter-agency meeting to discuss Special Education provision, and an application should be made that includes evidence of all the strategies and interventions employed to date.

How to help – tackling school refusal

☞ Tackle the problem as soon as possible. Don't cover up absences that you know are non-medical or unauthorised. Listen to the reasons your child gives for not being able to attend school. He or she might tell you about issues at school, or with peers. If there are family problems, be aware that they could be the root cause.

☞ Seek help from the school. Contact the pastoral care teacher, who will engage the help of the EWO or equivalent. Speak to your GP if there are signs that your child is distressed, anxious or displaying other symptoms of anxiety, and consider seeking a referral to Children and Young People's Mental Health Services (CYPMHS).

☞ If you can get your child into school to attend a meeting to discuss the problem, arrange to do this. If he or she will not enter the school building, try to find a neutral meeting point.

☞ Don't let your child do fun activities when he or she should be in school. Don't allow him or her to watch television, play games or behave as if every day is a holiday. Establish a routine around school day times – this will make returning to a timetable easier.

☞ Avoid getting into a bartering or bribing scenario. A reward system for positive things that are achieved is more effective and celebrates success, rather than causing more conflict when a bribe in return for promised progress has not moved anything forward.

Aim for a phased return to school – including a shorter day, and additional support to get into the building. Ask another trusted adult to help you with this, to share your burden and to negate the possibility of you yielding to emotional pressure at the school gate.

 Consider a different school. If your child expresses support for this, get help to achieve it. The new school should be made aware of the problem so that they can put support in place from the outset.

School refusal case study 1: Jacob

Jacob was in his second year of secondary school, with a history of patchy attendance at primary school. His attendance in his first year had been good, but within a few weeks of starting back after the summer holidays he was refusing to attend. His mother initially covered his absences, giving a series of medical excuses, but no serious condition was evident.

The Guidance Teacher alerted the Education Welfare Officer (EWO), and she arranged to make a home visit to investigate things. She reported back a series of concerns. It seemed that Jacob had a lot of control in the house and was able to manipulate his mother. She was a divorced single parent with two children. Her younger daughter was at primary school and attended well, but Jacob was resisting all attempts to get him to return to school.

In the meeting with the EWO, Jacob promised to attend school if his mother bought him a pair of expensive trainers. When she did that, he asked for equally expensive track trousers, and then a jacket. She bought all of these, and still he refused to attend. Jacob did not have a fear of school and did not exhibit signs of illness or anxiety. He appeared to have a very comfortable life at home that he was unwilling to give up – including daytime television and a games console in his room. He seemed to have no incentive to leave the house, and was not under any effective pressure to work at school.

The EWO established that Jacob had a good relationship with his paternal grandmother, who lived nearby. She was a strong character, and she agreed to work with Jacob's mum to get him back to school. She went to his house each morning to make sure Jacob was up, dressed and ready for school, and accompanied Jacob and his mother to the school gates. Jacob was collected from there by a teacher from the support Base, who escorted him into the building. He spent a few days full-time in the Base, to get back into a routine and to give him the chance to catch up on some of the work he had missed.

Jacob was phased back to all classes within two weeks. He re-established lapsed friendships, and also seemed happier at home. His attendance was tightly monitored by the school, and the EWO kept in regular contact with the Guidance Teacher. Jacob's grandmother continued to help her daughter-in-law and her grandson, and her support was invaluable.

School refusal case study 2: Emma

Emma was in her first year of secondary school, and had been identified by her primary school as a pupil who might struggle in the larger setting. Her parents met with the Guidance Teacher and discussed their concerns before the transition meetings. Emma was invited into the new school with her parents for a tour one afternoon when it was closed to other pupils, and her anxiety was evident then. She agreed to take part in group-work sessions during the summer holidays with other vulnerable pupils who would be in her year group, but only managed to attend twice out of six times.

Emma's attendance broke down quickly. All attempts to get her into school failed, and raised her stress and anxiety levels. The EWO supported her and her parents, and agreed to collect Emma each morning and bring her to the Base, where it was agreed that she would spend two hours before returning home. The plan was to build on this and phase her into classes over several weeks. She was introduced to some of her classmates, who came to work with her in the Base to show her what they were doing in their lessons.

Emma did manage to get into her English and Science classes, but the school was not successful in getting her beyond that. She had a breakdown at home, and it was agreed by her GP, the Educational Psychologist and other professionals at the school inter-agency meeting that a place be sought for her in a small, independent school on the outskirts of the city that had recently been established to work with fragile pupils. The local Education Department agreed to finance the fees, and she was enrolled there following a carefully managed transition period. She thrived in her new school, and remained there for the rest of her school education.

Chapter 14: Post-school options

Although many pupils look forward to their post-school life, for some young adults it can be a time of great anxiety and uncertainty. It heralds a huge change from the routines and certainties of school, and for some it can feel like a leap into the unknown. Often a pupil who has avoided, actively disliked or been disengaged from school will actually find it harder to leave – especially if he or she is unsure of gaining employment or being accepted into a college or university course. Feelings of uncertainty and low self-confidence can make it hard for young people to see much prospect of a future. They no longer have the comfort and security of school – even if they disliked it – and they are at risk of becoming increasingly disengaged from society and of developing mental health problems.

> **Key Point**
>
> *Although many pupils look forward to their post-school life, for some young adults it is a time of great anxiety and uncertainty.*

Schools should prepare pupils for leaving well in advance. They will have a clear idea of who is eligible to leave and when, and should target resources towards those who are approaching statutory age, in order to prepare them for employment, training or further education. Working with local colleges to offer part-time vocational courses can give pupils the skills needed to get into suitable employment, apprenticeship training courses or equivalent.

Work experience programmes are a valuable strategy for working with leaver groups. Health and safety regulations have made them harder to set up but, if possible, some sort of work experience – even if it is in a different field to the hoped-for destination – should be arranged. It has so many benefits, in terms of raising awareness of the world of work and improving self-confidence and self-esteem. All pupils should have access to the school Careers Service, and should be given one-to-one interviews to help them organise a plan for job-seeking, college or university applications. Mock interviews are helpful, and although young people often find them difficult at first, they benefit greatly from being put in a formal setting before the real thing. Peer evaluation boosts engagement and success with this.

The most difficult pupils to support in the last stage of their school career are the ones who have been disaffected for some time, or disengaged from the school through poor attendance or exclusion. It is vital that they are offered good careers guidance, and every effort should be made to get them into school for this. If this is not possible, the Careers Service will often still be available to support them outside school. If other agencies are involved with such pupils (e.g. youth workers or social workers), then there is a greater chance that they will be able to engage with the Careers Service.

How to help – planning for life beyond school

☞ Have conversations about life beyond school during calm moments when there is time to properly consider the subject. Trying to discuss your son or daughter's future at the dinner table with the whole family present may not be the best time.

☞ Allow your child to talk while you listen. Encourage consideration of a wide range of options, but let him or her as far as possible be in control. Remember, it is not your future and a young person who is pressured into a job or career is less likely to be successful.

☞ Use school reports to highlight areas of strength, and focus on these. Encourage your child to speak to the school Careers Service about career options, and if possible ask to be present at such interviews so you can better support your child going forward.

☞ Look for some work experience as part of the last year in school. Many schools offer or require this, but often the best placements are found through personal contacts, friends or family.

☞ Offer to assist with or check college, university or job applications. Encourage self-confidence, but help your child to appreciate the fact that many applications are never acknowledged and this is part of everyone's experience – it is not a personal rejection.

☞ If your son or daughter leaves school with nothing settled career-wise, encourage him or her to get involved in other activities, such as community volunteering, in order to get out of the house and stay mentally active. Young people can easily fall out of routine and lose any drive to get motivated. This is not healthy, and it can affect sense of self, wellbeing and long-term mental health.

Post-school options case study 1: Rhys

Rhys was a pupil in his exam year, who had a history of challenging behaviour and low-level disruption. He had older brothers who had also attended the school and had similar problems, and there was no real family incentive or support for him to be otherwise. Rhys was a likeable boy on a personal level, but he found schoolwork difficult and distracted attention away from that by behaving in a destructive way whenever he felt vulnerable. He was popular with other pupils, but seemed desperate to leave whenever he could. He worked well in practical subjects and was a star in his woodwork class, where he behaved impeccably.

Rhys felt that he had little chance in life, and he seemed sure that he would not find a job and would be on benefits, like his parents and siblings. He was referred to the Alternative Education Base when he was in his third year, and he had a self-referral card which allowed him to come out of class and into the Base to avoid confrontation and possible exclusion.

One of the Base Teachers was a former careers officer, and she worked with Rhys on how to complete applications forms, and on his presentation and interview skills. She managed to negotiate a work experience placement for him with a large joinery company in the city. They were so impressed that they offered him an apprenticeship when he left school. Even when they were forced to make staff cuts, they kept him on because of his excellent attendance, timekeeping and work ethic. He was the first person in his family to work, and was regarded by them as a bit of a novelty for that.

Rhys was Apprentice of the Year, and he qualified several years later. He would come back to visit the Base when he was on holiday, when he needed help with things (for instance, a passport or driving licence application), or when he simply wanted to let the school know how well he was doing. Rhys used the good relationship he had built with staff in the Base to completely turn things around at a crucial time in his life.

Post-school options case study 2: Florence

Florence was a confident, outgoing pupil in her exam year, who was well regarded by staff and other pupils in her year group. She was predicted to get a good set of results in her exams, but had no interest in staying on at school beyond statutory leaving age. She was keen to become a hairdresser, but her parents were not supportive of this. She used to say that she wanted to be a primary school teacher, and they were keen for her to stay on and apply to university to do this. They worried that she would not earn a good salary in hairdressing, and they doubted her commitment to it as a career.

Florence had worked as a 'Saturday girl' in a small local salon catering mainly for older people, and she had enjoyed her work. Still, her parents did not see hairdressing as a long-term option for their daughter. This resulted in both sides becoming entrenched, and Florence's mother contacted her Guidance Teacher to get some help and advice regarding possible career options. This meeting needed to be sensitively managed, with everyone's views being respected but Florence's opinions and choices remaining paramount.

Florence had spent some time in the Alternative Education Base when she needed emotional support after her grandmother's death, and she knew that one of the teachers there had been a careers officer. Florence asked her for advice regarding applications and college courses for Hairdressing, and she requested that the teacher attend the meeting with her mother, her Guidance Teacher and the school careers officer. At this meeting it was agreed that, before she made a final decision, Florence should try to get some work experience in a city salon, to ensure that this was indeed her chosen career path. She was keen to get experience in a larger, more diverse company with a clear training programme and a promotion structure.

The Base teacher used her contacts to get Florence some work experience in a top city salon, and Florence and her mother went for a pre-placement visit. Her mother was impressed by the variety of treatments offered by the salon, and she asked pertinent questions regarding training, salary and what a placement would involve. By the end of the meeting she was more supportive, although she still hoped that the placement might put Florence off applying for a traineeship, and that her daughter would return to school.

The placement was a success. Florence was offered a traineeship with the company when she left school, and she was delighted. Her parents accepted her decision, and they were supportive of Florence's chosen career when they saw how happy she was and how hard she worked to pass her skills tests in the salon and her professional qualifications at college. Florence remained with the company for several years as a qualified hairdresser, and went on to be a manager of one of their salons.

Part 4: Personal and health issues

Chapter 15: Illness and disability

The particular difficulties faced by young people with chronic illness are sometimes insufficiently acknowledged from a school perspective. They must often cope with a growing awareness of their condition and prognosis, and of its likely impact on their school life and beyond. They can experience a number of hidden losses – of their ability to kick back against their parents, of their freedom to rebel like many of their peers, and of their opportunity to make 'inappropriate' choices and take risks – which are all a normal part of being a teenager. They may also have mobility problems and rely on their parents for ongoing personal care (lifting, showering, dressing and so on).

> *Key Point*
>
> *Young people with chronic illness often see the gap widening between themselves and their friends, in terms of autonomy and independence.*

Although these young people may cope well with most aspects of the school curriculum and achieve good results academically, as they progress through their teenage years they can often see the gap widening between themselves and their friends, in terms of achieving autonomy and independence. This growing sense of loss can manifest in low periods and mental health issues, particularly in the later years of secondary school.

Young people who have been hospitalised for long periods of time due to medical conditions have much to deal with, and their return to school must be carefully managed – not only to support learning, but more importantly to provide additional emotional support that can be accessed on demand. These pupils often present as more mature than their peers, and more at ease in adult company. Yet they can often feel isolated because of their fears for the long-term future, and they often disconnect from social contact with their friends outside school.

Establishing contact with the young person and his or her parents at an early stage – well before enrolment in the school – and working together to agree a suitable care plan is essential. All school staff should be informed of the young person's condition and any emergency care procedures that are in place, and they should be kept abreast of any changes for the young person that might have an impact on his or her learning. Staff should also be aware of any siblings already in school, or who subsequently enrol, and keep in mind the impact on their lives of living with someone with complex needs.

Schools should recognise that there will be times when a young person with illness or disability might need more support in coming to terms with his or her situation or prognosis – especially as he or she gets older, and post-school discussions take place – or when he or she might feel more isolated or less independent than peers. The young person should be given a 'time-out' or 'self-referral' card to use at vulnerable times, allowing access not just to the school library but also to somewhere that he or she can engage with staff on an information basis and get one-to-one support if needed.

How to help – adjusting to illness and disability

☞ For both parents and schools, good relationships are crucial. Make contact well in advance of enrolment, and ensure that parents meet with staff who will support the child – including the pastoral care team, the medical team, and anyone who may be involved in assisting the young person to travel around the school building.

☞ Discuss the needs and expectations of all parties. Parents should share as much information as possible to ensure that the school has a clear picture of what is needed. Include the young person in all these discussions, unless there is a valid reason not to do so.

☞ Work together to draw up a care plan and make sure that all parties have a copy. Monitor and review this regularly and formally. Schools should know who is in the young person's friendship group, be alert to changes in this and conduct occasional 'friendship health checks'.

☞ Parents should keep the school updated on any important changes in medication, treatment or medical staff dealing with the child and his or her needs. If medication is held with the School Nurse or medical team, make sure it is replaced regularly.

☞ Try to allow the child as much independence as possible to avoid him or her becoming isolated from the peer group. Investigate groups that offer out of school supported activities, and explore the possibility of financial support for transport – including driving lessons if appropriate – to support increased independence.

Illness and disability case study 1: Isabelle

Isabelle had a degenerative physical condition that kept her out of school for much of the last year of primary education. She had undergone several big operations to try to give her more mobility, with the prospect of further operations over the coming years. From the outset the school was fully aware of the extent of her difficulties, and it worked closely with her parents to put a suitable care plan in place. Isabelle was always part of any planning meeting, and she participated fully in any discussions. She was mature for her age, and had strong opinions regarding what she needed to help her cope with all aspects of school life.

Isabelle had access to the team of classroom assistants. She was able to choose when and if she needed their support — mainly for getting around the building — and she formed excellent relationships with them. She was more at ease with older people and younger pupils, and there was some concern that she felt isolated in her own year group. This improved as she moved up the school and her peers matured. She had open access to the support Base — she registered there in the morning, and she had a locker where she could store her books and bag. Practical subject teachers made sure she had any equipment needed to allow her to cope in class, and they often donated extra equipment to the Base for times that she worked there.

Isabelle chose a reduced number of subjects for exams and used the Base for extra study. She formed close relationships with all Base staff, and she would help younger pupils who were having problems. When she reached her senior years, she would sometimes go through a bad patch — when her health issues made her feel depressed — and she was given intensive support at these times. Staff in the Base would engage her in art activities and allow her to be full-time there until she felt ready to return to classes.

The number of operations she was still to have prevented Isabelle from planning too far ahead, despite ongoing medical, social work and careers service support. She did achieve the grades that she needed for the college course she was interested in, and she got special consideration when she applied. She passed her driving test during sixth form and got a car through a 'motability' scheme. This allowed her much more personal freedom and independence outside of school, and it gave her a huge boost in confidence.

Illness and disability case study 2: Dylan

Dylan came to the Base when he had just come out of hospital. He was in his fifth year of secondary school, aged sixteen, and he had been diagnosed with cancer following a sport injury that would not heal. After a partial amputation, he was easing back into school. He was full-time in the support Base, until he felt he could return to his classes to prepare for his exams.

He presented initially as a laid-back, cheerful young man, but this was very much a veneer. The Base staff got to know Dylan and his family well, and he started to speak openly about his experience and his fears. He was not discussing things at home – he was very protective of his parents and his younger sister, and he did not want to increase their grief – and he had changed his friendship group, so he had no main confidante. Previously he had mainly socialised with his sport team-mates, but he felt that he could no longer do that – even though they were keen to see him. He spent much of his time out of school with other teenagers he had met in hospital. Some of them died, and he felt sure that this was going to happen to him. He stopped working for his subjects, became more withdrawn at home, began to drink heavily and admitted to behaving recklessly when he was out.

In school, Dylan was given a self-referral card, open access to the Base at breaks and lunchtimes and one-to-one support whenever he needed it. His timetable was reduced to just subjects he enjoyed and was likely to work for, and the additional time was spent on artwork in the department. He was linked with a male youth worker who could address some of his more personal and long-term issues. The school liaised closely with the care team from the hospital, and his support worker visited Dylan in school so that they could discuss any problems or concerns. A priority for Dylan was to be able to look ahead with hope – to a future out of school and with good health. He expressed a wish to become a chef, and the member of Base staff who had once been a careers officer negotiated a special work experience placement with a Michelin star chef who had a restaurant in the city.

One-to-one support was also offered to Dylan's sister in school, but this was on a more structured basis and at a time when he was not in the Base. This was an important piece of work, because staff knew that she was struggling and needed the opportunity to vent her feelings in a safe environment with staff who could see her at short notice if she was feeling upset, or fragile.

Dylan left school in better health, although still not fully recovered, and he managed to get a training position in a small hotel restaurant near his home.

Chapter 16: Mental health

A significant percentage of pupils are diagnosed with mental health issues during their time at secondary school, and this is increasingly identified during primary or even early years education. Indeed, the transition from primary to secondary education can itself be a traumatic experience, and lead to a rise in anxiety levels.

> **Key Point**
>
> *Schools must develop strategies to allow young people with mental health difficulties to remain in education and work towards resilience.*

Levels of local authority expertise and support for young people with mental health difficulties will vary significantly, and underfunding can often lead to long waiting lists for group, family and one-to-one interventions. It can be hard for a young person to hear that they are on a six- or even twelve-month waiting list; this can seem like an excessively long time to them, particularly as they are already distressed, and it often means that parents and schools must try to manage such issues themselves, at least in the short term. In particular, schools must develop strategies to allow young people with mental health difficulties to remain in full-time education and to work towards building resilience and good long-term wellbeing.

Jennifer Spratt and her colleagues drew on a Scottish study for a 2006 article discussing the impact that the school environment can have on pupil wellbeing.[5] They suggested that schools should draw on the experience and knowledge of inter-agency workers to provide an integrated rather than a parallel approach to care, and that there should be whole-school staff training on mental health and its importance. Teachers who notice significant changes in a pupil's behaviour, attainment, friendship groups or mood should alert pastoral care staff and provide as much detail as possible about their concerns, and pupils known to be struggling should be offered a place of safety – where they can self-refer for respite or in an emergency, but also where they can continue as far as possible with their normal classwork.

---

5 Spratt, J., Shucksmith, J., Philip, K. & Watson, C. (2006) 'Part of Who we are as a School Should Include Responsibility for Well-Being': Links between the School Environment, Mental Health and Behaviour, Pastoral Care in Education. 24 (3): 14-21 (https://doi.org/10/1111/j.1468-0122.2006.00374.x)

For pupils with known mental health issues, there should be a pre-enrolment meeting with parents/carers and the young person, in order to familiarise them with the school and to address any concerns. A plan of action should be agreed, and all teaching staff informed. As well as a family referral to the GP, the pupil might benefit from a referral for one-to-one support from a youth worker or other agency (where available) who could offer support on a regular basis. A referral to Child and Adolescent Mental Health Services (CAMHS) should be made to support the young person in the long term, in conjunction with medical support via the GP.

Some young people live with parents or carers who themselves have long-term mental health and/or dependency issues, and it is hugely important that these young people feel supported in managing the expectations of school, balanced against the realities and challenges of their lives at home. More discussion of pupils who are also carers can be found in Chapter 30.

How to help – sharing mental health concerns

☞ Inform the school as soon as possible of any known or diagnosed mental health issues. Speak to your child about any new concerns he or she has, and discuss coping strategies and what he or she may need help with, in order to maintain good wellbeing in school.

☞ If you are concerned that your child is becoming anxious, withdrawn, has mood changes, is self-harming or is abusing substances, you should contact your GP in the first instance. Your child may not wish you to be present at the appointment; but getting him or her there in the first place is the important thing.

☞ Contact the school pastoral care team to discuss any concerns, and ask for a meeting. There will probably be signs that all is not well in school. Try to get your child to attend this meeting if he or she is able, but don't apply too much pressure. Keep your child informed of any discussions, and of any plans to help him or her in school.

☞ Discourage your child from staying away from school. This can lead to further isolation from the social aspect of school, which is important. If helpful, provisions can be put in place – such as a safe place to go for respite, or a means to ask for help in a crisis.

Mental health case study 1: Lily

Lily came to secondary school with known mental health issues. Although she was able to manage well most of the time in school – with the support of her peers – it was considered likely that the transition from primary to secondary education would be traumatic for her.

The primary transition meetings allowed the primary school class teacher who knew Lily best to liaise with the Guidance Teacher who would work with Lily at secondary school. They both met with Lily and her mother in the secondary school to agree a plan, let them look around the building and give them the opportunity to ask any questions. On the induction visit, two sixth form pupils were assigned to 'buddy' Lily, guide her around and answer any immediate questions or concerns.

When she started in her first year, Lily was accompanied around the building by a classroom assistant who was attached to the class specifically for her. Staff were made aware of Lily's health issues, and they took extra care to monitor her wellbeing and progress. She settled in well, and seemed to enjoy the new school environment. She was given a self-referral card to the support Base to use if she felt anxious, but was encouraged to be in class as much as possible. She was closely monitored by staff, and she met regularly with her Guidance Teacher. When Lily was making her course choice for her third year it was agreed to limit her timetable, and that she would join the reduced timetable social skills group in order to increase her practical skills, boost her confidence and help her build resilience for the future.

Mental health case study 2: Noah

Noah was referred for support when he started his fifth year, at the age of sixteen. He had managed to get good year four results, but his mother was alarmed by changes in his mood and behaviour over the summer holidays. He was isolating himself from friends, staying in his room, not eating or sleeping properly, and seemed upset or anxious. He had seen his GP, who diagnosed him with depression and prescribed anti-depressants.

Initially, Noah returned full-time in the Base, but he negotiated a return to all subjects within two weeks. Staff were made aware of his medical issues and gave him leeway regarding workload and homework deadlines. He established excellent relationships with all Base staff, and benefitted from one-to-one counselling, a self-referral card and individual youth worker support. He was referred to Children and Young People's Mental Health Services (CYPMHS) for family counselling sessions and one-to-one support. His health and confidence improved greatly over time, and he volunteered as a Base helper before leaving school to take up a college place.

Chapter 17: Self-esteem

It is almost impossible to underestimate the power of self-esteem as a positive or negative influence on young people. We really do need to consider each individual's situation and recognise that problems, and sometimes negative behaviours, may be rooted in low self-esteem. Pupils who do not engage with staff, or who are noticeably withdrawn or excessively confrontational, are often actually lacking in confidence, and their coping mechanism is their 'front' – the image they present to the world.

> **Key Point**
>
> *Pupils who do not engage with staff, or who are noticeably withdrawn or excessively confrontational, are often actually lacking in confidence.*

Ironically, the image presented by such individuals can be of someone who seems overly confident, so low self-esteem is not the first thing we think of as an explanation for their behaviour. It can be hard to think of difficult behaviour as a sign of self-esteem problems; it's quicker and easier just to categorise a person as a troublemaker. Yet, as in many situations, the quick and easy route is not always the one that will lead to growth in our approach, or in the person we are dealing with. We need to keep reminding ourselves that we could be seeing the young person's negative self-image projected outwards. It is always better to start by giving the benefit of the doubt, and to look for ways to explore and improve the young person's self-esteem.

In order to identify potential problems at an early stage, parents and carers should be alert to any changes in mood, behaviour, eating or sleeping patterns. If problems are suspected or behaviour issues are reported, then talking to the young person in a calm manner, in a non-punitive atmosphere and at a time when he or she is not upset or anxious is always the best way. Avoiding school is never a good idea, as avoidance can quickly become a coping mechanism and hinder the development of long-term resilience.

How to help – harnessing the power of self-esteem

☞ Identify any pupils with self-esteem issues as part of the primary transition process. Parents should alert schools as early as possible. Ensure that pupils with self-esteem issues are placed in classes with at least one good friend, and monitor their progress.

☞ Arrange for pupils with known issues to receive additional support as part of their induction – small group sessions pre-transfer to address concerns and work on confidence and friendship skills, with follow-up sessions during the first term in secondary school.

☞ Work closely with parents to encourage the young person to take part in extra-curricular and social activities. Set short-term, achievable targets/goals, and draw up an individual achievement chart so that the young person has evidence of his or her progress.

☞ Include self-esteem, confidence and team building in the school's social education programme, and revisit this regularly. Celebrate success for all pupils with a positive referral system, whereby all staff can acknowledge personal achievements.

☞ Acknowledge underlying self-esteem issues for pupils who have behaviour issues in school. These are best dealt with on a one-to-one basis with the pastoral care teacher or youth worker, using counselling, target-setting, close monitoring and a reward system.

Self-esteem case study 1: Isla

Isla's primary school class teacher had many concerns about her transition to secondary school. She was quiet at school, often withdrawn, and had difficulties forming and keeping friendships. She was not excited like most of her peers about moving to her new school, and she was becoming increasingly anxious about this. Her mother reported that Isla's behaviour at home had deteriorated and, if challenged, she would refuse to leave her room or have temper tantrums which were excessive in their intensity. She had a very positive relationship with her primary school class teacher, but there were concerns about attachment issues and low self-esteem.

When the school transfer arrangements were being made and the Guidance staff came to visit pupils in Isla's primary school, her teacher flagged these concerns and strategies were put in place both for the induction visit (which took place in the secondary school over three days, just before the summer holidays), and for the first few months of Isla's time in her new school. Isla and her mother were invited to have a meeting with the member of staff who would be her Guidance Teacher before the induction visit, when the school was closed to other pupils. They were able to walk round the school, visit some of the classrooms and see where the social areas for new pupils were located. Isla was encouraged to write down any questions she might want to ask after the meeting, so that her mother could email them to the Guidance Teacher in the hope of allaying any new fears.

Isla was allocated to the same class as her closest friend and a few others from her primary class, to give her some continuity. On the induction visit, she was allocated a sixth form pupil to be her 'buddy'. This pupil was attached to the whole class, but had been briefed regarding Isla and another vulnerable pupil who might need additional support for the visit. Isla was brought to the support Base and introduced to staff, to let her see where she could come if she got a bit lost or was feeling anxious. She was then taken to meet the School Nurse, who had also been alerted to her anxieties.

Isla was referred for a summer holiday group run by the school youth worker to support pupils who were anxious or who had low self-esteem. This group met weekly in the school to work on team building, self-esteem and confidence. The young people were also given one-to-one support in order to deal with individual concerns before the start of term, and the group continued during term time to address any further transition issues.

Isla's Guidance Teacher monitored her progress closely in school, and met with her and her mother to review progress. Isla settled in well, and when she was in her fourth year, she became one of the pupils who went out with staff on primary transition visits, to reassure other anxious young people.

Self-esteem case study 2: Liam

Liam had a history of bullying behaviour at primary school; however, he had shown little evidence of this in his first year at secondary school and it was felt that he had managed the transition well. He seemed settled and happy until the spring term of his second year, when preparations were underway for subject choice with the prospect of increased work pressure. He became unsettled and less cooperative, and he received several punishments for poor behaviour. However, it was his behaviour outside the classroom that raised more serious concerns. He had started to bully other pupils in his year group, and especially those who would be regarded as vulnerable. He was identified as the ringleader of a group of pupils who had attacked a younger pupil on his way home from school, and he was formally excluded for this.

Chapter 17: Self-esteem

On his return to school, Liam maintained a low profile for a few weeks but then a group of girls in his class – who liked him and had had always had good relationships with him – reported to their Guidance Teacher that he was making obscene comments about them, and had drawn offensive graffiti about one of them on a wall in the cafeteria area. Liam admitted responsibility for the comments and graffiti, but would not engage in any dialogue regarding his reasons for suddenly turning on the girls who had previously been his friends, and who were clearly upset by his behaviour.

Liam's mother was called into school to discuss this, and she provided the Guidance Teacher with additional background information that had not previously been fully disclosed. She was a single parent – she had given birth to Liam when she was sixteen, and she had no contact with his father. She had been in an abusive relationship with another partner when Liam was at nursery school, but this ended when there was a Child Protection inquiry following unexplained bruising on Liam's body which was noticed by a nursery teacher helping him to get changed for swimming. Nothing was proven, but there were concerns that this partner had abused Liam when his mother had been at work. Other bruises had been explained away by this man as falls or accidents, or as carelessness on Liam's part.

Liam's mother had hoped that things had settled, but agreed that other agencies needed to be involved to offer Liam support, and to address his behaviour towards other pupils. Liam was discussed at the inter-agency Pupil Support Group. It was agreed that a referral would be made to the Educational Psychologist, and that he would also be referred to mental health services for one-to-one support and family counselling. He was identified as having self-esteem issues that had gone unresolved for years, but which were causing him pain as he progressed through adolescence.

Liam was referred for one-to-one anger management in the Base to look at his behaviour in classes and towards his classmates, and to help him deal with changes in mood, which could be sudden and overwhelming. He also took part in some group work sessions with other pupils identified as having social skills needs. These involved organised play sessions to look at interaction and cooperation. It was noted that Liam found it difficult to play, and that he could not relax in a play environment but would choose instead to fight or kick out, or deliberately spoil a game for others. He would not engage in group work discussions, and was unable to complete a simple paper exercise based around personal skills and positive qualities.

Liam's lack of self-esteem and confidence became the focal point for support work with him. He had one-to-one support for the next two years from a male mental health worker, who provided him with a positive role model and someone he could confide in about events of the past. He and his mother benefitted from family counselling sessions, and their relationship improved greatly as a direct result. Liam was also supported for the rest of his years in school by the staff in the Base, and by his Guidance Teacher. In his fifth year, he volunteered to be part of the Peer Education Programme, where senior pupils, working alongside staff, acted as tutors and mentors and offered a level of additional support to struggling first-year pupils.

Chapter 18: Sexual health

Sexual health is an important and integral part of general health, and should therefore form part of the social education of young people from primary school through to the end of secondary education. Research carried out in England in 2006 by Jo Westwood and Barbara Mullen[6] found that while older pupils were better informed than younger pupils about sexual heath, in all age groups knowledge about sexually transmitted disease and emergency contraception was poor. They concluded that current sexual health education was not providing adequate information in these areas.

> **Key Point**
>
> Young people need information and support to develop good sexual health and an understanding of relationships based on consent, trust and respect.

Young people need information and support in order to develop good sexual health and an understanding of relationships based on consent, mutual trust and respect. Every school should have a clear, comprehensive and well-developed sexual health programme that is taught in an age-appropriate way across all year groups. It should cover physical and sexual relationships, health and wellbeing, contraception and all aspects of sexual health awareness – sexually transmitted diseases, HIV/AIDS, responsible decisions and respect for diversity. Contemporary information around sexual health, contraception and pregnancy should be included. Schools should ask pupils for feedback each year, and act on it. This can result in a topic being dropped into a younger year's programme, so that it is not 'too little, too late.'

Schools should also have a clear commitment to teaching pupils about Lesbian, Gay, Bisexual and Transgender (LGTB) and intersex rights, and a clear approach to tackling homophobia and transphobia. In 2019, Scotland became the first country in the world to make this teaching compulsory, to embed it in all aspects of the curriculum, and to support all LGBT young people and adults in the school community.

Staff from external sexual health education agencies can sometimes offer invaluable, credible programmes in schools, particularly with senior pupils who do not always want to discuss sensitive issues with pastoral staff. These agencies also have up-to-date resources and use young staff

---

6 Westwood, J. & Mullan, B. (2006) Knowledge of secondary school pupils regarding sexual health education, Sex Education, 6 (2): 151-162 (DOI: 10.1080/14681810600579121)

as their main trainers, which tends to be a successful approach in terms of engaging meaningful discussion. All external agency staff will have cleared the relevant disclosure checks that anyone working with young people must undergo. Pupils should be made aware of health agencies that can support them out of school, and an up-to-date list and/or leaflet board of relevant organisations and helplines should be made available in the school.

Anyone working with young people in a professional capacity will be fully aware of the legislation around Child Protection and their obligation to deal with all disclosures in accordance with national guidelines, without exception. These guidelines will typically state clearly what constitutes verbal abuse, emotional abuse, physical abuse, inappropriate sexual activity, sexual abuse, statutory rape and other abuse, including online grooming. They will have clear lines of referral around who should be involved in heading up any investigation of a disclosure, and what forms of action should be taken in order to protect the young person(s) involved as a matter of urgency, as well as to deal with perpetrators through the legal system. Education, social work, health professionals and police will provide a coordinated response to any disclosure, and their level of involvement will be decided on a case-by-case basis.

How to help – a positive approach to sexual health

☞ Find out what the school's sexual health education programme is for your child's year - schools should make details available via the school handbook and website. Some schools offer an information evening to allow for discussion and questions, and to make parents fully aware of Child Protection guidelines and procedures.

☞ Be aware of your child's sexual health, and encourage them to have a positive, open attitude and to see it as part of their overall health. Ask your child what is being discussed in health education at school, and listen to the answers. Be ready for your child to ask difficult questions, and refer to online information if helpful.

☞ Encourage your child to have a healthy attitude towards sexual health, and to see it as part of their overall health. Stress the need for mutual respect in all relationships.

☞ Research the school's LGBT teaching and its support of young people in the school community – again this should be in the school handbook and on the website. Any concerns around discrimination, prejudice or bullying should be reported to staff immediately.

☞ If you have concerns about your child's sexual behaviour, risk-taking behaviour or possible abuse, ask clear, non-judgemental questions before taking any action. Try not to overreact to what you might find out. Keep all discussions calm, safe and supportive.

☞ If you have concerns that your child is involved in unsafe, abusive or non-consensual behaviour, don't try to manage it alone. Seek help from health professionals, police, social workers and other agencies available. Make it clear to your child that any action taken is to protect his or her long-term general and sexual health.

Sexual health case study 1: Matthew

Matthew was a pupil who presented as either cooperative and enthusiastic about school and life in general, or confrontational and subject to mood swings. He was popular with other pupils, especially girls in his year group who saw him as a good support if they had personal problems. He was an excellent communicator, and acted as a mediator and go-between to seek advice for a friend who was unable or unwilling to approach staff.

Matthew had come out as being gay in his second year, and he did not experience problems about this from his peers. His father was another matter altogether. Matthew's parents had separated when he was in primary school and, although he had had regular contact with his father, he saw less of him in his teenage years. This was because of his father's homophobia and offensive personal comments, and because his father blamed Matthew's mother for their son's sexuality. Matthew's mother was fully supportive of him, but also aware of the struggles that Matthew had in dealing with his father's disapproval. Contact with his father was often followed by low mood, poor behaviour in school and a drop in attainment.

Things came to a head for Matthew when he was sixteen, at a meeting with his father and his Guidance Teacher, where his father was abusive and dismissive of his son's school report and Matthew's plans for his future. His father's manner was aggressive and confrontational, and as a result the meeting was terminated. It was agreed with Matthew, his Head of Year and his Guidance Teacher that no further meetings would take place in school involving his father, and that Matthew's mother would be the only parental contact regarding report cards and any other personal issues.

Matthew received additional in-school support from a youth worker, and self-referred to a city LGBT support group. He represented his year group on the school council, where he proved to be an excellent communicator and an effective advocate for other LGBT young people in school. He continued to do well academically, achieved good grades and left after his fifth year to work in an office in London. Several years later he returned to education, completed a degree in Social Work and became a teenage youth worker.

Sexual health case study 2: Fourth year pupils

A group of fourth year pupils in the school population were identified as being involved in serious risk-taking behaviour in the community, including alcohol and drug use and under-age sexual activity. Although the school had an age- and stage-appropriate sexual health programme in place as part of social education, and pupils were fully aware of Child Protection guidelines and issues regarding confidentiality, there were no disclosures; however, enough was said or implied to initiate discussion in Guidance and pupil support meetings about the need to offer more targeted work in school.

Many of the young people about whom staff were concerned had attendance and behaviour issues in school, so any work needed to be planned carefully, delivered sensitively, and not seen as judgemental or a trap to elicit disclosures that might lead to Child Protection intervention. The Guidance and Alternative Education teams, working with the multi-agency Pupil Support Group that included a community police officer, agreed to offer a programme covering identified areas of concern. It was felt that this should be led by youth workers as they would be seen to have a level of 'street credibility' and conversations would therefore be more candid than if school staff were present – although pupils would be made fully aware that the Child Protection rules still applied without exception.

Pupils were recruited through their Guidance Teachers, and numbers were restricted to ten pupils in a mixed-gender group. Work was done to explain the group's aims, and it was agreed that it would meet in one of the support Base rooms initially, with visits to other health and community resources once the group's rules and programme had been agreed. Parental permission was sought for pupils to be part of the group, and the youth workers offered to meet with any parents who wanted more information.

This group ran for twelve weeks. It covered all aspects of sexual health, and much of the programme was developed and agreed following issues raised within the group. The young people who took part were positive about it, and reported that they had been made more aware of the dangers of risk-taking behaviour and the need for them to regard their sexual behaviour and long-term sexual health more carefully. Their comments about the school's sexual health education programme were fed back to staff, and this informed changes that were made to the programme for the next iteration.

Chapter 19: Eating disorders

Anorexia nervosa, bulimia nervosa and other forms of eating disorder are devastating and potentially life-threatening conditions. They are symptomatic of serious emotional problems, and are very difficult to overcome. In 2003 Frédérique Smink and colleagues carried out a review of the prevalence of the two most common eating disorders, and found that on average 0.3% of young females (three individuals in every thousand) suffer from anorexia, and 1% (one individual in every hundred) suffer from bulimia.[7]

> *Key Point*
>
> Life is harrowing for those who suffer from eating disorders, and it can be even more so for the families trying to keep someone they love alive.

Life is harrowing for those who suffer from eating disorders, and it can be even more so for the parents and families trying literally to keep someone they love alive, and to reach a point where they can once again trust that person with his or her own health. Although both anorexia and bulimia centre on eating and body image, they differ in the ways in which they are recognised and managed. They are not restricted to females, although most cases that receive media attention suggest this. For example, the research study mentioned above found the male prevalence of bulimia to be 0.1% (one individual in every thousand), although it seems that young men who suffer from eating disorders are often reluctant to speak about it openly.

There is often felt to be a greater urgency around anorexia than around bulimia, because the symptoms of anorexia mirror those of starvation and there can be a rapid decline in body weight. It is more obvious to people who know the sufferer and it can disrupt the normal life of a young person, to the point where immediate hospitalisation is the only means to prevent death. Bulimia can be hidden or masked for longer; many people suffering from bulimia can track their illness much further back, and it can shock close family members when they disclose their condition. This is because bulimia involves a cycle of bingeing and starvation – so there may be few outward signs of illness, and those that do exist might be explained away as other illnesses. However, bulimia is just as serious a condition as anorexia, and early diagnosis is crucial to avoid decades of future problems.

---

[7] Smink, F.R.E., van Hoeken, D. & Hoek, H.W. Curr Psychiatry Rep (2012) 14: 406. (https://doi.org/10.1007/s11920-012-0282-y)

It is likely that parents will be the first to suspect that their son or daughter may have an eating disorder, either because of physical changes or because their child is frequently being sick or having bouts of diarrhoea. Other warning signs that should trigger alarm bells are shown in the table below.

How to help – eating disorder warning signs

 Anorexia

- A preoccupation with body weight and image, and a negative self-image
- Avoidance of family meals and excuses for not eating – claims of having eaten already, or not liking the food presented
- Arguments around not finishing food – presenting an excuse to storm off and therefore avoid eating or any discussion
- Having a restricted group of 'safe' foods that can be calorie-counted and that look like more on the plate than they are
- Cooking or baking for others, but not joining them to eat
- Rigid rules around what to eat, when and how much
- Outward signs: thin appearance, tiredness, low mood, mood swings, irritability, poor circulation that can induce a blue tinge to the skin, always feeling cold, changes to thickness and shine of hair, dry and flaking skin, problems with teeth, swelling of joints, menstruation problems, dizziness, increased facial hair with a soft, downy appearance
- Increased exercise – often immediately after eating – and outbursts of temper if over-exercising is not possible
- Wearing baggy clothes, often several layers, to hide weight loss
- Refusal to take part in PE in school, to avoid detection
- A reluctance to take part in family events where people might comment on changes, or present other challenges

 Bulimia

- A preoccupation with body weight and image, and a negative self-image
- Frequent comments about being fat, ugly, or both – having a distorted view of his or her weight
- Reluctance to eat in front of others, or a tendency to eat slowly and without enjoyment; anger if challenged about this

- Binge eating of what the person would regard as 'bad' foods
- Purging – either self-induced vomiting or the use of laxatives in large quantities after binge eating
- Strict dieting or fasting after a period of binge eating
- Exercising excessively
- Outward signs: fluctuating weight, mood swings, problems with teeth, frequent sore throat from vomiting, swollen glands and face, increase in soft, downy facial hair

Within a school, all pastoral care staff will have a good awareness of eating disorders, but whole-staff training is valuable in highlighting that this is something that will almost certainly affect several young people in any school population. Staff should be encouraged to alert pastoral care colleagues if they notice any changes in a young person that might indicate an eating disorder. PE staff can be particularly helpful in this – perhaps because of physical changes, but also because the pupil might be reluctant to take part in any activity that involves revealing his or her body shape.

All schools should have a clear healthy eating policy. Healthy eating should be discussed as part of PHSE (Personal, Health, Social and Economic) education classes or equivalent – along with body image, media portrayal of body image and peer pressure. These subjects can also be discussed with pupils as part of the broader curriculum in several subjects.

If the school is made aware of a child having an eating disorder, staff should work closely with the young person and his or her parents to agree a strategy to allow the young person to manage in school. There should be an inter-agency meeting with the young person (ideally) and the parents or carers present, to agree a plan of support, and to agree who is doing what. There should be monthly updates and future meetings scheduled to involve any medical, mental health, youth worker or psychological services staff.

The pastoral care teacher should liaise closely with the school medical team to discuss how best to support the young person, to monitor problems or concerns and to update the young person and his or her parents at regular review meetings. Note that school staff cannot and must not be put in the position of being responsible for monitoring or controlling a young person's eating, and this should be made clear to parents or carers. It would be an unreasonable expectation, and it would not succeed. If the young person agrees, he or she should have access to a quiet area to have lunch with a few friends, but without feeling that he or she is being spied on.

If a young person has been absent from school for some time, then a phased return is likely to be required, or a part-day timetable where normal classes are combined with a respite area for catching up and one-to-one support. Flexibility with deadlines is important, but pupils should be encouraged to complete work whenever they can. It may be that some young people would benefit from foregoing exams to focus on their health, but this decision should never be taken lightly. Many young people with eating disorders are high achievers and should be supported to fulfil their academic potential as far as possible, although the stress that can accompany exams should be anticipated and discussed as part of a whole-person approach to care.

How to help – identifying and managing eating disorders

☞ Don't turn mealtimes into battles – you will not win.

☞ Don't jump to conclusions if a child is losing weight – it might just be part of the many changes involved in adolescence. Don't ignore warning signs if they are starting to add up, but tread warily: people with eating disorders will often deny they have a problem, and become angry and withdrawn (thereby retaining control).

☞ Find out all you can about eating disorders, and seek medical help. This can be a long-term condition, and if help is not sought until a late stage it will not be an easy fix. You will require support for yourself and other family members, especially siblings, to cope.

☞ Choose a calm time and a private setting to discuss your concerns with your child. You might find this easier when both parents are present, but if one parent is likely to get angry or upset, or has a better relationship with your child, take this into account.

☞ Listen to what your child says. Don't just counter-argue; try to discuss negative comments and acknowledge feelings. Then you can work towards a plan or an agreement about what you can do, who should be involved and how quickly it can be done.

☞ Avoid making the conversation about you and your emotional response. Instead, ask questions to try to get your child to explain what his or her perceptions are.

☞ Do not bombard your child with dire warnings of where an eating disorder can lead – he or she is probably more aware of the facts than you, and unlikely to change because of your fears.

☞ Inform the school. Speak to your child's pastoral care teacher, and put strategies in place such as removing your child from PE and allowing time out for tiredness. Make sure the school nurse is aware of your child's condition, and can monitor things closely.

☞ Try not to let this issue dominate your family's life. If you have other children, ensure that their lives are not taken over by it. There is a risk that siblings can feel resentment, or less valued in the family.

Eating disorders case study 1: Ellie

Ellie was in her fifth year of secondary school and a high achiever, clearly set for university with a plan to study Medicine. She had been diagnosed with anorexia the previous year and had had long periods of absence, including one spell of hospitalisation to stabilise her weight. She was on a positive trajectory, but she needed additional support in school to give her respite during the school day, and to allow her access to members of staff she trusted. Her timetable was reduced to take out PE and one other subject that she could drop without affecting her university application.

Ellie was articulate, fully conversant with her condition and managing much better since her discharge from hospital, where she had received excellent emotional as well as physical support. The problem came when she signed up for a foreign school trip to France and her mother was reluctant to let her go. The trip involved four days touring World War I battlefields, followed by two days in Paris. Her mother agreed that she could go on the trip, but she asked if a member of Base staff could monitor Ellie's eating and make sure she finished meals. This was still a real bone of contention at home. The mother was told that this could not be done – it would ruin the trip for Ellie, for the member of staff and for others, and it would isolate Ellie from the group. It was also unlikely to be effective, because Ellie might find a way to get rid of the food by purging or avoiding mealtimes altogether.

Ellie did come on the trip. She knew that the member of staff had refused to monitor her, and made a point of subtly letting her know that she had eaten (albeit small amounts) at each meal. She enjoyed the trip and continued to spend time in the Base until she left school for university. She stayed in touch with the Base for some years, and visited the school occasionally during the holidays. She would never describe herself as 'cured', but said her eating disorder was like an addiction that she could now control. She spoke about the support she'd received, and felt that this had been well-managed and that she had a voice. She qualified as a surgeon several years later.

Eating disorders case study 2: Grace

Grace was referred to the Base during her fourth year of secondary school. She was returning after an absence, where she had been diagnosed with bulimia and put on medication. She met the Head of the Base with her parents, but she was sullen and angry and refused to participate much in the discussion. Her parents were exhausted: her father was unable to come to terms with the fact that his beautiful daughter believed that she was ugly and hated herself and, while her mother was more able to be supportive, the strain on them both was palpable. Grace had a younger brother who was in his second year at secondary school, and who was affected by the tension in the house. He was unable to bring friends home because of this.

Grace had been a dancer and gymnast, but she had given up both activities because of her poor body image. She was beginning to avoid her friends. She identified another girl who had made derogatory comments about her, and she felt that these comments were the root of her decline into bulimia.

It was agreed that Grace would reduce her school timetable, focus on her exam subjects, and have a self-referral card for the Base. Her parents both worked full-time, so one of the Base staff arranged to collect her from home each morning (she lived near the school). She agreed that her medication would be held by the member of staff, who would give it to her each day. She seldom missed school, but there were days when she was clearly low. Mondays were particularly bad, because she had often binged and purged at the weekend, and felt weak and low at the start of the school week.

Although Grace did reasonably well in her fourth year, the challenges continued and she continued in the Base in her fifth year. She also joined an English class taken by the Head of the Base; this meant that she could be monitored in a key subject, and also that her relationship with that teacher was not always defined by her illness. She would frequently say that she was going to leave school, but she had agreed with the Base staff that no decisions could be made on 'bad' days, so that did not happen.

Grace was supported by her family GP, whom she trusted and who was a huge support. The GP had referred her to Children and Young People's Mental Health Services (CYPMHS), who provided some family counselling and one-to-one sessions, but Grace did not find these helpful or frequent enough to make a difference. She left school with fewer qualifications than she was capable of, but got a job working for a large organisation in one of their central offices. Her true ability was soon recognised by her managers, and she was promoted several times over the following few years. She became someone who was training graduate-entry staff at the age when she would have been one of them, had she gone to university.

Though Grace's eating disorder was still a factor in her life, it became less debilitating. She left home, became independent of her parents, and took control of her eating. She married, had children and now leads a normal life.

Chapter 20: Self-harm

Self-harm is a common problem that impacts a significant number of young people of all ages, but it is most evident during the teenage years. In 2009 Rory O'Connor and colleagues collected information from more than two thousand pupils in Scotland, and found that 13.8% of them reported having self-harmed at least once.[8] Approximately the same prevalence has been found in England. Girls were around 3.4 times more likely to report this than boys. In both boys and girls, factors associated with self-harm were smoking, bullying, worries about sexual orientation, self-harm by a family member and anxiety. Among girls physical abuse, drug use, serious relationship problems, self-harm by friends and low levels of optimism were also associated with self-harm. The authors concluded that schools could provide support in emotional literacy, and that they should promote positive mental health

> **Key Point**
>
> Young people self-harm to feel in control, or to relieve tension. The pain gives some release, but it puts them into a cycle of harming behaviour.

School medical and pastoral care staff will be aware of self-harm as an issue, but they may not be aware of all cases as much self-harming is hidden and kept away from adults. Self-harm can include cutting, burning, pulling out hair, scratching or picking at the skin. It is primarily a way of dealing with emotional pain, anxiety and depression – usually a reaction to stress, bullying or a traumatic event. Young people self-harm to feel in control, or to relieve stress or tension. The pain of their injury gives some release, but it puts them into a cycle of harming behaviour that is distressing for parents and carers and becomes difficult to break without professional help.

The following are situations where young people are at high risk of self-harm:

- Problems within the family – e.g. abuse, conflict, separation, divorce
- The young person feels isolated or rejected
- The young person has mental health problems
- The young person has an eating disorder

---

8 O'Connor, R., Rasmussen, S., Miles, J., & Hawton, K. (2009). Self-harm in adolescents: Self-report survey in schools in Scotland. British Journal of Psychiatry, 194(1), 68-72. (doi:10.1192/bjp.bp.107.047704)

- The young person is also abusing drugs or alcohol
- Another family member or close friend self-harms

Schools should ensure that all staff are aware of self-harm as an issue that will affect a significant number of young people, and should include this in PHSE classes or equivalent for all year groups. Class teachers should report any concerns about possible self-harming behaviour to pastoral care staff. PE staff are often the ones who first notice frequent or unexplained injuries, along with a reluctance to remove clothing for physical activities and/or a refusal to take part in activities. Some young people might disclose concerns about a friend to a pastoral care teacher, or to a favourite trusted teacher. If this happens then they should be supported, and time should be spent trying to ensure that the friendship does not fall apart as a result.

Once self-harm is evident, either because of an in-school concern or because a parent or carer has informed the school, a pupil-centred meeting should be arranged to look at supports that can be put in place. The resulting plan of action must be one that the young person can agree to – otherwise, it simply will not work. The family GP will need to be involved, so the school's key role is to support the young person's emotional needs. As part of the plan, clear rules must be established around self-harming behaviours in school, in order to protect other young people and to make the young person take responsibility for their own actions and behaviours.

The young person should have access to one-to-one support, a self-referral card to a safe place for vulnerable times, and perhaps a quiet area set aside for a few friends to eat lunch together if he or she cannot cope with large groups of people. This avoids isolation and provides a positive focus to the day in school, which may be one of the key stresses. The young person should be referred to an inter-agency group in school to discuss any other supports that can be put in place, as well as other agencies that may be able to offer support for out of school hours, weekends and holidays. If there is a youth worker attached to the school, he or she may be able to offer one-to-one or group work sessions to work on self-esteem and coping strategies.

How to help – recognising and managing self-harm

☞ Be aware of the warning signs – unexplained cuts, burns or other wounds and an unwillingness to discuss them; hair loss; reluctance to uncover arms or legs, even in hot weather; refusal to take part in PE or other physical activities in school; painkillers or other medicines going missing from the medicine cabinet; carrying small, easily concealed sharp objects; spending long periods alone and becoming more withdrawn; mood changes; low self-confidence.

☞ If you believe that your child may be self-harming, speak to them – but only when the situation is calm, and in a non-confrontational manner. Do not express shock or disgust; convey your concern for their welfare and the need to work together to make things better.

☞ Discuss who to ask for help – but insist that help is sought. You cannot manage this alone, and your child is unlikely to be able to stop just because he or she has promised to do so. Self-harm is indicative of serious emotional issues that must be addressed. Also get support for yourself from a friend or trusted family member.

☞ Contact your GP, who can give immediate care if necessary and refer your child to other supports including mental health provision.

☞ Inform the school and arrange a meeting with the pastoral care teacher. Discuss supports available in the school, including referral to the school medical team. This should be a pupil-centred meeting with agreed strategies and a review date set.

☞ Agree 'house rules' with your child to protect other siblings, and to acknowledge the risks within the home. Do not keep large packs of medicines, and keep prescription medicines locked away.

☞ Be prepared for lapses in your child's ability to stop the cycle of self-harm. Treat any new injuries calmly, in the same way as you would any other form of accidental injury. Seek medical help if the injury is serious, but stay positive for the longer term.

Self-harm case study 1: Amelia

Amelia was in her second year at secondary school and, depending on her mood and her opinion of each teacher, was either excellent in class or extremely difficult to manage. She would go through the school week on a rollercoaster of emotions, seesawing between punishments and positive referrals from staff. After a particularly fraught week, where she faced temporary exclusion from classes for behaviour issues, she disclosed to her Guidance Teacher that one of the reasons she was not coping was because she was self-harming, and she felt that this was getting out of control.

Amelia's home situation was erratic. Her father had recently been released from prison, but his return to the family home was not going well. He had been violent to Amelia's mother in the past, and Amelia was concerned that this might happen again. Her mother had an alcohol dependency problem that was under control while her father was away, but Amelia felt that this was not going to last either. She felt negative about her home life and had low self-esteem and body image issues. She also had few close friends, although she was popular in class.

Things came to a head for Amelia when she realised that her PE teacher (one of her favourite teachers) was growing tired of her excuses for not participating in class, and the prospect of further confrontation was just one stress too many. Fortunately, she was keen to get help with her self-harming. A plan was agreed with her Guidance Teacher before her mother was asked to come into the school. At the meeting, which involved Amelia, her mother, the School Nurse (who Amelia knew well and liked) and the Guidance Teacher, several things were agreed:

- Amelia's mother would make an appointment for her with her GP and be present at the meeting – with Amelia's consent
- Amelia's father would not be told, as this was likely to raise other issues; Amelia was adamant about this
- Amelia's case would be discussed at the inter-agency meeting in school, to explore other support strategies for her
- Amelia would check in with her Guidance Teacher after main school registration each day, to discuss any problems or likely issues
- Amelia would not take part in PE for a few weeks until her cuts had healed; when she returned, she could wear leggings and long sleeves
- During the missing PE time she would work in the Base, catching up on work and receiving one-to-one support on an ad hoc basis

Amelia asked if either the School Nurse or the Guidance Teacher could check her arms and legs each day. She felt that this would be a good incentive not to self-harm. The School Nurse gave her advice regarding things to do to distract herself when she felt vulnerable, or likely to harm herself.

The school worked with Amelia for several months, and, despite one serious lapse which coincided with her father leaving the family home permanently after a domestic abuse incident, she made good progress. She was referred for one-to-one youth worker support, which ran during the term time and through the school holidays. By the time she reached her third year, she felt much more positive about things and was no longer self-harming.

Self-harm case study 2: Fredek

Fredek enrolled in the school for his fourth year. His father had been made redundant, and the family had moved from abroad so that he could take up a new job. Fredek was upset and angry about the move. He hated being in a strange city and a new school, but particularly hated where he was living. The only house they had been able to get was in a disadvantaged area, and he resented this having previously been quite indulged materially. The changes in the family's circumstances had devastated him, and he withdrew almost completely from any meaningful relationship with his parents.

Fredek was bright, articulate and made friends easily, but he gravitated towards a disaffected group of pupils in his year and soon began truanting classes and staying out late at night. His parents were unable to discuss anything with him without it becoming a confrontation. They discovered that he was self-harming when he came home so drunk that he had to be undressed for bed. Fredek's self-harm – carving words on his arms and legs – was copying the behaviour of a member of his favourite band, who had discussed his self-harm in the media. Fredek was direct and open about this, and his parents were frantic, especially when he refused to see his GP.

Fredek's mother contacted the school to inform them of what she and her husband had discovered, and a meeting was held. Fredek was open about his cutting, was keen for people to see his scars, and would roll his sleeves up when he was in classes. Although there were some concerns about the attention-seeking aspect of this, the priority was to look at the emotional causes – and at who could become involved in supporting him.

Fredek was discussed at a school inter-agency meeting, and the school medical services became involved. It was agreed that a referral would be made to Children and Young People's Mental Health Services (CYPMHS), and that he would get one-to-one support from the male school youth worker, with whom he had a good relationship. He was given a self-referral card for support in the Base, on the understanding that he must not miss classes at any other time and that this would be monitored closely. He had to use Base time to catch up with work to keep him on track academically. Strict rules were put in place around self-harming in school, to protect other young people.

Following an argument with his parents at home one weekend, Fredek self-harmed quite seriously and the injury required hospital treatment. His parents had called the police as well as an ambulance, as they were concerned for his mental health. They were terrified that he would take his own life, as he had threatened to do this several times. He was admitted to a young people's psychiatric ward, and was a patient there for almost a month. He received intensive support and counselling, but he was not considered to have a psychiatric illness and so was discharged and referred for family counselling.

Fredek went through several months of ups and downs, including periods of relapse, but worked hard to overcome his difficulties. He succeeded in completing his exams, and he did well enough to earn a place at university.

Chapter 21: Dependency

Secondary schools, like the rest of society, are well aware of the increase in dependency issues among teenage pupils – spanning everything from alcohol and substance abuse to social media addiction and gambling. Drugs, alcohol and other forms of addiction should be discussed with young people of all ages as part of PHSE or equivalent, and staff awareness of dependency issues should be part of ongoing whole-school training.

> *Key Point*
>
> *Schools are well aware of the increase in dependency issues among teenage pupils – spanning everything from alcohol to social media.*

If a school becomes aware that a pupil has a dependency issue, the first step in tackling the problem is to offer support to the young person and his or her parents or carers via a pupil-centred meeting in school to acknowledge issues and address concerns. Everyone should have their say, but the meeting should end with clear agreement around what has been decided, what supports the school can put in place, and what else might be required from outside agencies engaged with the school. A follow-up inter-agency meeting should be arranged to formalise issues and plan support both inside and outside school. It should be clear who will take responsibility for each agreed action point, and a review date should be set.

It may be helpful to draw up a contract for the young person. This can often focus targets, avoid agreement that only lasts until he or she leaves the room, and provide a useful reference point for weekly discussions. If a young person is given a 'self-referral' card for support facilities, or extra leeway from staff regarding deadlines and homework, this should be monitored and regular feedback sought from teachers for each formal review.

Depending on the young person's age and where they are on their school journey, there may be merit in reducing his or her timetable and arranging for other activities to be put in place. This could involve peer support of other pupils, working within a subject department where the young person does well and has a good relationship with staff, or work experience outside school. Such activities can often remotivate young people and give them a sense of achievement. Whatever is decided, support should also be offered to any siblings of the affected young person in school. This can be low-key, but it is important that their welfare is also recognised and monitored.

How to help – confronting dependency

☞ Be aware of dependency issues among young people. Accept that some risk-taking behaviours are common in teenagers, but be alert to when things go beyond experimentation, or when your child is not coping – when there are changes in mood, habits, sleeping, behaviour, school attendance, attainment, motivation and so on.

☞ Discuss things calmly with your child. This is no easy task, but to do otherwise will only result in stalemate and hostility. If you can, list your concerns – not as a series of accusations but as undeniable evidence of change. Then there is more chance of a real dialogue.

☞ Make it clear that you cannot contain these issues alone – you will have already tried this – but that you all need help to cope. Make sure you have already investigated what help may be available to you. This will vary by place, but you should be able to find up-to-date information online, from your doctor or from the school.

☞ Contact your GP as soon as possible and inform the school of your concerns. Staff may already have some knowledge of these issues, but a meeting should be held to discuss how they can help. This should be pupil-centred, and not be seen by your child as punitive.

☞ Put firm rules in place at home. These should be agreed as part of a calm, negotiated discussion with your child, so that there is a clear understanding about what is acceptable. If rules are broken – as is likely – avoid having discussions at flash points as they will not achieve anything and are likely to make things worse for everyone.

☞ Accept that progress may be in small, slow steps, but acknowledge any successes and encourage your child to get involved in activities that change their routines. Be creative with this. Ask for help from friends and family members with whom your child gets on well.

☞ Engage as fully as you can with any external agencies or individual youth and community workers who might become involved in supporting your child – but accept that much of their work will be confidential (within Child Protection guidelines or equivalent).

Parent dependency

Alongside addiction problems suffered by young people themselves, there is also an increasing issue for teens who have a parent or parents with a long-term dependency problem. Such problems may well be common knowledge in the community, and these young people are often put in the position of being young carers and keeping their parents on an even keel while trying their best to 'parent' other siblings. This robs them of their teenage years and inevitably leads to problems with school attendance, attainment, social interaction and mental health. Education often ends up last on the list of priorities. More information on young carers can be found in Chapter 30.

Young people in this situation may receive support from friends' parents or other adults in the extended family, but their feelings of isolation and loss cannot be underestimated. They are unlikely to reveal the true extent of their daily situation – family loyalty can be a powerful force – so it is vital that schools offer intensive support, a safe environment and a degree of stability, and allow the young person to have a voice.

If a pupil comes to the school with known parent dependency issues, there should be careful handling of the transition and every effort should be made to have a meeting with the parents, the young person and any professionals already involved in their care. The young person should be placed at the centre of any school supports, and care should be taken to match him or her with a suitable pastoral care tutor. This person should be included in all transition meetings from the outset, as young people can get very defensive if they are asked to repeatedly share their story with new professionals.

If dependency issues are not known about in advance, they may be revealed after concerns about the attendance, welfare or changes in the young person's mood or attainment. Sometimes they are revealed through comments made by other pupils, which cause pain or upset to the young person. If staff are made aware of any of these things, they should flag up their concerns to pastoral care staff in the same way that any other Child Protection issue would be passed on.

Whenever a parent dependency issue is recognised, there should be an inter-agency meeting to ensure that all relevant agencies have been involved and to look for additional support for the young person and any other siblings (who may be at other schools or nurseries). Consideration should be given to out of school hours, weekends and school holidays, when young people affected by this issue can become totally isolated. In school, there should be provision for one-to-one pastoral care, a self-referral process for additional support at stressful times, and flexibility regarding workload and deadlines built in across the curriculum. Additional help with career decisions and university applications should also be available, with the possibility of positive discrimination policies for these areas.

Dependency case study 1: Ryan

Ryan was in his first year, and had come to secondary school with a long history of family problems, behaviour management issues and also some learning difficulties, all identified as early as nursery school age. He lived with his father and a younger sibling (aged two) in impoverished conditions. His mother had died the previous year from an accidental drug overdose, and his father was a (barely) functioning addict who received social work support to allow him to keep custody of his children. This was proving difficult for everyone involved: Ryan was anxious about leaving his father each morning (he would make breakfast for his father and sister, then only come to school if he felt things were likely to be all right for the rest of the day). His father was often unable to cope, and did not have a network of other adult support. His social worker would sometimes be refused entry to the house, other than to take the younger child to a day carer.

Ryan's behaviour in school was often confrontational, and few sanctions worked – as indeed had been the case in primary school. His Pupil Progress Report reflected the intensive support that had been required to maintain him in school and to actively avoid exclusions. His needs were multiple and complex. He was undernourished for his age, and was described as a 'failure to thrive' child who often came to school hungry and poorly clothed for the weather conditions. He was often absent, usually late, never completed homework and would not accept normal class discipline. He would openly defy teaching staff in order to be excluded from classrooms, and gravitated towards the support staff in school: the School Nurse, his Guidance Teacher, the Support for Learning staff and the Alternative Education staff.

Ryan was discussed at the School Liaison Group on numerous occasions, to look at alternative strategies to allow him to be maintained and supported effectively in mainstream education. He was in danger of further exclusion, and was seen as being at risk in the community. He was also becoming more socially isolated within his year group, and he mixed with older pupils – in their third and fourth years – who also had behaviour issues in school. The following supports were quickly put in place to help:

- Ryan reported each day to the Alternative Education Base, regardless of arrival time, to allow him to get settled and registered and to have something to eat and a hot drink. He was also encouraged to have school lunches which were partly supervised by staff.
- He was issued with a daily Conduct Sheet with targets for that day that he would agree with a member of staff. This was not sent home to be signed by his father, as it was acknowledged that it would not be looked at or returned so it would have no value for Ryan.
- A reward system was agreed for good days, with the emphasis on setting realistic targets and addressing problem subjects and times. Ryan was not issued with a self-referral card for the Base, as it was felt he could not cope with this and would miss more class time.
- Regular meetings were held in school with Ryan's family social worker, to review the home situation and to discuss school issues. He was also given one-to-one youth worker support during school holidays, to monitor the home situation and to provide focus for each day by linking him with community-based activities.

Matters escalated when Ryan's father collapsed at home after a drug overdose and Ryan and his sister were taken into care. It was agreed that future contact with their father would be on a supervised basis only, and that the children would be fostered together in a family on the other side of the city. This was set to be a long-term placement, so an inter-agency meeting agreed that Ryan should be enrolled in a school near his new home, with intensive transition support put in place. Ryan was initially reluctant to make this move, but it was dealt with sensitively. He was encouraged to keep in touch with the staff that he saw as his supports in his old school, and he was given intensive support in his new school. He maintained contact for a few weeks, until this dropped away naturally. He was someone who would need ongoing intensive support throughout the rest of his young adult life.

Dependency case study 2: Amy

Amy's mother was an alcoholic who had been through several rehabilitation programmes. She had been involved in a serious car accident in her early twenties, and had sustained some brain damage. Her alcoholism was attributed in the family to her inability to fully recover from this accident and having little prospect of being able to hold down full-time employment. She had received a large sum of money as compensation for the accident, and there was concern that this had attracted the attention of a group of people who were regarded as a bad influence on her for years afterwards.

Amy had no knowledge of who her father was – her mother had given her various names of who he might be, but nothing had been addressed regarding the truth of this so Amy had given up hope of getting an answer. Amy's mother was from a good, supportive family who lived in the local area, so Amy's health and welfare were managed mainly by them. She often stayed with her maternal grandparents or one of her maternal aunts or uncles. She was particularly close to her mother's older sister, who she felt was better at keeping her mother 'in line' regarding her drinking.

At primary school, Amy had been supported well and presented as an enthusiastic, well-integrated child. The transition from primary to secondary school was well managed, but things started to unravel towards the end of her third year. Amy's mother's health deteriorated – she had a new partner who was also a heavy drinker – and and Amy spent more time living with relatives away from home. More worryingly, Amy herself was picked up several times by the local police for being drunk while socialising with older teenagers in the park. She was abusive and aggressive, and she was visibly distressed when taken to her grandparents' house.

Concerns about a deterioration in Amy's attendance record, poor behaviour towards some staff and underachieving in classes brought things to a head in school. Amy was anxious that she was destined to become an alcoholic like her mother, and she felt that in some way it was pre-programmed in her genes. She expressed strong feelings of helplessness and hopelessness, and she had clearly reached a crisis point.

A Pupil Support Group meeting was held to review Amy. Her aunt attended in place of her mother, and several supports were put in place:

- Amy was referred to the Alternative Education Base for one-to-one work to look at the school-based issues, and she was issued with a self-referral card to give her respite on difficult days and at times when she might otherwise truant classes or not attend at all.
- An emergency referral was made for social work support. Amy was also referred to Alateen (part of Alcoholics Anonymous), a recovery group for adolescents who have relatives who are alcoholics and, for those whose lives are negatively affected by it.
- It was agreed that Amy would spend weekends at her grandparents' house and the rest of the week with her aunt. She would only visit her mother if she had assurance that she was not drinking, and this visit would be restricted to two hours after school. She would not stay overnight unless this had been agreed with her social worker.
- Amy was given clear, agreed targets regarding attendance and attainment – something she welcomed and that she felt she could work towards – to get her back on track in school.

- Amy was encouraged to return to a running club held in a local sports centre which she had belonged to for several years, but which she had allowed to lapse when she began to socialise with older teens.

Amy benefitted from having a clear, well monitored plan of action, but also from having a very supportive, tight-knit family network. She managed to maintain a reasonable relationship with her mother, who continued to drink and was unwilling to engage in another rehabilitation programme. They were both realistic about the unlikelihood of Amy ever returning home. Amy's social worker supported her in trying to get some clearer answers regarding her biological father, but was unsuccessful in resolving this.

Amy managed to get a good set of exam results, and took up employment as a trainee hairdresser following successful work experience in a city salon.

Part 5: Interpersonal issues

Chapter 22: Friendships

Secondary schools generally get their first-year intake from a number of feeder primary schools in the local area, and the newly formed classes will be a mixture of individuals from these various schools. For many pupils, a new school means the excitement of new friendships – but for some there can also be the pain of old friendships changing or potentially coming to an end. This can result in a huge amount of upset both for pupils and for their parents or carers, as well as for staff in the new school, and it is an area that must be handled sensitively.

> **Key Point**
>
> For many pupils, a new school means the excitement of new friendships – but for some there can be the pain of old friendships coming to an end.

It is crucial to take the time early on to listen to any concerns that children may have, and if things don't settle over time to liaise with the school so that a practicable solution can be found. Friendships and transitions should be explicitly addressed by the school. This will pre-empt many of the issues that can arise, and create the conditions required for ongoing discussion of interpersonal relationships. This in turn demonstrates to pupils that friendship is something that should be taken seriously, and it helps them to develop social skills that will of great value to them throughout their lives.

Early in a school year, schools should monitor new intake classes closely and identify any pupils who are vulnerable or who seem to be having problems with friendship changes. Teaching and support staff should be asked to alert pastoral care staff to any concerns about group dynamics, or about specific pupils who appear to be struggling to settle. Older pupils can be used as 'buddies' in the early weeks (although this should only be short-term as the older pupils will have their own work pressures to deal with), and trusted pupils in a class can be asked to include a pupil who is feeling isolated from break and lunchtime groups. This strategy usually works well if negotiated and monitored carefully, but do not force things if it does not work.

Friendships and other issues around transition should be discussed in PSHE classes or equivalent, and case studies can be used to encourage group discussion. Issues of falling out should be dealt with in a non-punitive, constructive way; this always works better than trying to apportion blame for what is a normal part of the transition process.

In-school group work involving social skills, teambuilding and outside activities could be considered for pupils who seem to be particularly quiet and/or withdrawn. If an individual pupil continues to struggle, the school should liaise with his or her parents to get their perspective, and to agree strategies that might help.

How to help – friendship groups and issues

☞ Listen to what your child says about new friends or friendship groups at school, and expect there to be a level of disruption and change. Allow time for this to settle down naturally.

☞ Don't tackle other children or their parents; this seldom works. Raise any concerns with your child's pastoral care teacher. He or she might well have identified issues within a class or friendship group already, and may be speaking with other parents.

☞ Encourage your child to invite new friends over for tea or to socialise – but don't apply pressure or push this too hard. Follow your child's lead in terms of what he or she is comfortable with.

☞ Try to interest your child in joining after school sports or activity groups, as these can often be where new friendships are formed.

☞ If, after a few weeks, you still have concerns, discuss them calmly with your child, and try to identify the issues. Don't magnify the issue, get angry or demonise other children. Remember, most of these issues will resolve themselves after a settling-in period.

Friendships case study 1: Emily

Emily found the move to secondary school difficult. Although she was in a class that included some pupils she already knew, she didn't have a close friend and felt isolated from all the newly formed friendship groups. She felt that she was being sidelined by some of the more powerful girls in the class, and she began to be withdrawn and miserable at home. Her parents noticed that she was particularly low on Sunday evenings, and that she often complained of an upset stomach or headache on a Monday morning.

Careful questioning at home revealed Emily's concerns. She agreed that her mother could contact her Guidance Teacher, who alerted Emily's teachers to keep an eye on her and include in her in class groups where possible (usually by the teacher choosing groups rather than pupils self-selecting). She then approached a small group of supportive girls in the class and asked them to look out for Emily and include her whenever they could. The pupils did this sensitively, and Emily's life in school improved. Before long, she was an integral part of the friendship group – and later she was the one to step forward and befriend a new girl who joined the class from another country.

Friendships case study 2: Daniel

Daniel's mother was anxious that her son was not making new friends after starting at secondary school, and she contacted the Guidance Teacher to discuss her concerns. She had been encouraging Daniel to invite new friends over to the house for tea, but he refused even to discuss this with her. She was worried that he was becoming isolated, or even that he might be being bullied. After careful questioning by the Guidance Teacher, however, she conceded that he was not displaying any genuinely concerning behaviours at home, and nor was he avoiding school. He was not presenting any problems in school, and staff reported that he seemed perfectly happy in class.

The Guidance Teacher had noticed that Daniel tended to spend his breaks and lunchtimes with two other quiet boys in the year group (who were in different classes), and that they shared similar interests in cars and technology. It seemed that Daniel's mother was projecting her own expectations and experience of being part of a large and lively friendship group on to her son, and this pressure was what Daniel found annoying. He was perfectly happy with his chosen friends, and he enjoyed school. Daniel's mother agreed to stop pressuring him, and instead to let him be himself.

Chapter 23: Bullying

Bullying is probably the issue that most parents would put at the very top of their list of potential concerns about their child's life at school. Certainly that is the authors' experience, based on many years of working in educational contexts and with parents.

Bullying abuse can take many forms:

- physical – threats of violence and actual attack
- verbal – insults, name-calling, teasing (which is a matter of interpretation)
- racist
- homophobic
- online and social media (cyberbullying)

In 2000, Derek Glover and colleagues investigated the incidence and impact of bullying in twenty-five secondary schools in England.[9] This included physical bullying, verbal bullying and property violation behaviours. They found that in any given secondary school year, 75% of pupils are likely to be bullied to some extent, and 7% of pupils are likely to experience severe and repeated bullying.

> **Key Point**
>
> Bullying is probably the issue that most parents would put at the very top of their list of potential concerns about their child's life at school.

The research team concluded that if intervention is to be effective, then it should involve tackling attitudes both in pupils and in the wider community, and that there should be a greater understanding of and respect for personal space.

Bullying, then, is an issue in all schools, just as it is an issue in many workplaces and organisations and even within families. Every school and Local Authority will have a clear, detailed bullying policy, with guidelines and recommendations, and schools must make pupils and their parents fully aware of their content on enrolment. Bullying should also be a topic of discussion in PSHE classes or equivalent, and all pupils should be encouraged to report any bullying they suffer or witness to a member

---

9 Glover, D, Gough, G., Johnson, M. & Cartwright, N. (2000) Bullying in 25 secondary schools: incidence, impact and intervention, Educational Research, 42:2, 141-156, DOI: 10.1080/001318800363782

of staff. All teaching staff should be trained to identify different forms of bullying and respond appropriately both within their classroom and in the wider school. There must be a clear referral route for staff to report bullying to pastoral care staff or the school's Senior Management Team for urgent attention.

For many cases of bullying, there will be a clear plan of response based on:

- the type of abuse
- the relationship between the victim and the abuser (if one exists)
- the intent of the abuse
- the details of the incidents – frequency, severity, ongoing threat
- the feelings of the victim – the need for counselling, support, meeting with the victim and his or her parents/carers
- investigation of the abuser – the need to get full background details; meeting with the abuser and his or her parents/carers
- punishment – reparation
- restorative meeting – if appropriate and agreed with the victim and the abuser

However, each case must be handled individually, and often a creative approach, within the parameters of the guidelines, is more effective than a catch-all method. A fine tightrope must be walked. It is best to let pupils lead the way, and the hardest thing about this is often that the approach may not satisfy the desire of parents to punish the perpetrator as a primary aim. However, if parents or staff take immediate action without the consent of the young person being bullied, and they get it wrong, then the young person is very unlikely to bring any other concerns to them in the future.

If a case of bullying is identified, pastoral care staff should work closely with the young person and his or her parents or carers, always allowing the young person to lead the way. He or she may initially not want any action to be taken at all, or may agree only to limited action that does not involve his or her identity being revealed to the bully. If the victim is certain of the perpetrator's identity and wishes action to be taken, then the bully should be spoken to by his or her pastoral care teacher. The parents should be informed and formally invited to the school to agree a plan of action that might involve punishment, sanctions or a restorative meeting with the victim led by a member of staff. The bully might also be referred for support to deal with issues of anger and/or violence.

If the bullying is serious, persistent or escalates out of school, the matter should also be referred to the police and formal exclusion from school should be considered to protect victims while a long-term solution is sought. If the school has a community police officer, then he or she can be very helpful in cases of this kind. More generally, community police officers can work with pastoral care staff to deliver bullying information as part of PSHE classes or equivalent. They may also be able to lead restorative justice initiatives, and meetings in school that set out to resolve sensitive issues.

How to help – addressing bullying problems

☞ Listen to your child, gather as many details as possible, and discuss the situation calmly. Do not immediately rush to the school or make any contact with the perpetrator(s) or their parents.

☞ Work on a plan together, but allow your child to be in control. Do not give your child bad or outdated advice – fighting will never be tolerated in a modern school as a response to bullying behaviour.

☞ Discourage your child from staying away from school. This seldom resolves the problem, and it often makes the situation worse.

☞ Establish an understanding of school policy and procedures around bullying, and contact your child's pastoral care teacher to discuss matters (ideally with your child present) and agree a way forward.

☞ If the bullying is also taking place online, you should contact social media providers who have a duty to remove offensive material. Further discussion of cyberbullying is provided in Chapter 24.

Bullying case study 1: William

William, a pupil in his second year of secondary school, was seen hanging around after school one day. A Guidance Teacher spoke to him, and it seemed he was reluctant to leave and had contacted his mother to come to collect him. This aroused the Guidance Teacher's concerns, and also worried William's mother. When she arrived the teacher asked her and William for a quick meeting, and William reluctantly revealed that he was being bullied by a boy two years above him. There was no apparent reason for the bullying – he had no past with the boy, and only knew his first name. The older boy had been targeting him at lunchtime when he was with his friends at a local shop.

The Guidance Teacher recognised the boy from William's description, and she asked William how he wanted to proceed. They could wait to see if the bullying stopped (not really a viable option, but it had to be put on the table), tackle the older boy as a result of a formal complaint from William, or tell the older boy that a member of staff had seen him bullying an unnamed younger pupil and reported it. William chose the third option, and the Guidance Teacher spoke to the older boy the following morning.

The older boy had a history of disruptive behaviour in classes, but he was usually pleasant on a one-to-one basis. He admitted to picking on William, but he had no awareness of the impact his actions were having on the younger boy. He agreed that he had problems controlling his temper at times, and he agreed to being referred for in-school anger management support. He offered to apologise to William, but William refused this. He just wanted the bullying to end, and for his school life to get back to normal.

Bullying case study 2: Jessica

CJessica was part of a powerful group of girls in their fourth year at secondary school who were well known to staff and other pupils. In a classroom setting Jessica could be difficult to manage, disruptive and verbally abusive to staff. Many pupils were entertained by her, but many were afraid of her too. She was regarded as the leader of the group, and although efforts were made to separate them in classes, it was not possible to keep them apart at breaks and lunchtime when their impact was most felt.

Jessica was reported for bullying other pupils on several occasions, and she had been through the discipline route for this with little effect. She had had one-to-one Guidance support, youth worker support in a group setting and anger management in school – which had made an improvement for a while. She had been excluded from school three times, and she was now in danger of permanent exclusion. Her mother was a single parent with younger children, and she was afraid that her daughter was going to end up with no qualifications. However, she was unable to effect any change.

After another complaint of bullying, Jessica was discussed at a school inter-agency meeting, which she and her mother attended. It was agreed that they would apply for temporary hosting in another school. The school's hosting coordinator approached the other local schools to see if they had an available space, and if they would be able to offer Jessica a similar course of study. Two schools offered a place, so Jessica and her mother chose the one that suited them best in terms of travel to and from school.

Jessica's first eight weeks in her host school were unsettled at times, but she was less disruptive and worked better in classes. After a second eight-week block, she was offered the chance to enrol permanently. She chose to return to her original school, but on the clear understanding that she had to make it work or she was in danger of permanent exclusion. She managed much better on her return, continuing her anger management and successfully completing a work experience placement. With support, she saw out the rest of her time in school successfully without any further exclusions.

Chapter 24: Cyberbullying

Online bullying, or 'cyberbullying', is any form of harassment that takes place using electronic devices, such as mobile phone and computers, where people are involved in social media and where content is shared or viewed by others. It can involve the sending of sensitive or personal content as well as false, derogatory or malicious information which causes upset, humiliation and embarrassment, or the sense of threat to someone else.

> **Key Point**
>
> *Cyberbullying is any form of harassment that takes place where people are involved in social media and content is shared or viewed by others.*

Much information that is posted online is permanent, for all practical purposes, and can only be removed if reported. The fact that young people live much of their lives via their phones and computers and use social media so much increases the chances of them being affected by this form of harassment. This is a concern not just for parents, but also for schools and the school community – where the fallout can result in conflict, anguish and emotional and psychological harm for the victim. This can ultimately affect school attendance, educational attainment and self-confidence.

Cyberbullying can be very subtle, and it can be difficult for parents and schools to recognise or identify it. It is often only discovered once things have progressed to an almost unbearable point for the young person affected. Schools should include online safety and security in training for all staff, and as a topic within PSHE or equivalent for all year groups. A clearly articulated and justified policy on the use of phones in school will ensure that parents and pupils are aware of restrictions and the reasons for them. Monitoring the use of mobile devices in school is important (but tough!).

Schools should be alert to any changes in the behaviour of a young person – attendance, mood, attainment or friendship group – and any 'throwaway' comments by other pupils about social media gossip. A zero tolerance policy on all forms of bullying should of course be standard practice, but instances of cyberbullying should be dealt with as a matter of particular urgency.

How to help – promoting online safety

☞ Familiarise yourself with what social media is, what it does and what the risks are. Search online, ask other parents and ask your child (he or she will probably be the most up to date!).

☞ Support school policy on the use of mobile phones in school hours; and discuss expectations around your child's use of electronic devices and social media before it becomes a problem.

☞ Make sure your child is aware of the difference between 'just for a laugh'- type comments that they might post about other people, and when a line is crossed into bullying and harassment.

☞ Watch for changes in your child's behaviour and mood – especially after using phones or electronic devices – and encourage him or her to discuss any concerns about communication received that is upsetting or troubling.

☞ Act immediately if you feel that online bullying is taking place – it can escalate much faster than other types of bullying. Stress the need to have comments removed, and change settings to prevent any further communication from the perpetrator(s).

☞ Save any evidence you have, with times and dates. Do not retaliate, but block the person who is sending offensive communications and report the bullying to the site provider.

☞ If the bullying is from a peer group source, inform the school immediately to alert them to the likelihood of this spilling over into the school environment.

☞ If the cyberbullying involves threats of physical violence or threats to safety, or is of an explicit or sexual nature and/or involves photographs that invade privacy, contact the police.

Cyberbullying case study 1: Lauren

Lauren, a high achieving pupil, coped well with the demands of secondary school and had a strong friendship group. She was a volunteer in the Alternative Education Base for part her fifth year, working to deliver a peer social education programme to a group of vulnerable first-year pupils who were finding school life difficult. Her closest friend, Sasha, had been with her in primary school, and they had stayed together in several classes in secondary school, both working towards university application.

Lauren seemed to have no problems with her life at school, but she arrived at the Base one Monday afternoon highly distressed following a 'joke' that Sasha had posted on social media the night before, without Lauren's knowledge or permission. By the time Lauren got wind of it, the post had been in the public domain for more than twelve hours.

A pornographic photograph of an unknown female had been altered digitally and Lauren's face had been added, with comments implying that she had behaved outrageously at a party her group of friends had attended at the weekend. This image had been sent to her friendship group, then copied and circulated to a much wider audience. Abusive messages were coming directly to her phone and computer – many from people she had never even met – and there was nothing she could do to stop it. She felt humiliated, hurt and unable to be in school, certainly not to attend classes, and she could not understand why she had been victimised and abused in this way.

The decision was made that immediate action was required to deal with this matter in school, and to support Lauren who could not envisage returning. An emergency meeting took place with Sasha and her parents, and the details of the false image and the rationale behind its circulation were discussed. Sasha was initially defensive and dismissive of what she saw as Lauren's overreaction to a joke, until she was spoken to by the school's community police officer, who had dealt with similar issues in the past.

Both sets of parents were involved – they too were friends – and the reality of the situation was spelled out clearly. Understandably, emotions were high, so it was agreed that Sasha would not be allowed back into school until the matter was resolved to Lauren's satisfaction. Lauren would work full-time in the Base until she felt ready to return to classes. The matter would be dealt with by the police, leaving the school in a purely pastoral role, which included discussion of online bullying with all year groups in PSHE classes.

Lauren's parents contacted the social media site provider on the advice of the community police officer. Sasha removed her original post then issued a statement regarding her 'joke' and a public apology to Lauren. It would never be possible to delete all copies of the image, but the apology was also posted on by other people. As part of a restorative justice initiative, the community police officer set up meetings with Lauren and Sasha to discuss all aspects of this act of bullying and its consequences. Lauren felt that she had been given the chance to have her say, to listen to Sasha's side and to express her feelings. The friendship did not survive this incident, and Lauren removed herself from the social media group – as did several of her friends.

In this case, both the victim and the perpetrator were known to the school – and to each other. Increasingly, with the rapid advance of technology and the rise of 'trolling' where people can remain anonymous, cases of online abuse are much harder for police and other watchdog agencies to monitor and control. This will increasingly be an issue for young people in school, and one that schools cannot resolve as they do within their own community.

Cyberbullying case study 2: Amal

CAmal was in his fourth year at secondary school and played for a local football team. He hoped to be taken on by one of the larger city clubs; he had already been approached and was being monitored. He and his football teammates started a group chat on a social network, initially to organise training and to discuss their shared interest in football. The players attended four different schools, but they socialised after training and matches at the weekend. Following a defeat against another local rival team, where Amal had scored an own goal, one of his teammates posted an abusive comment about him, angrily blaming him for the team defeat, and others joined in.

Although there were a couple of comments from other players who tried to joke about things and calm the matter down, over the next few days the comments became more aggressively abusive. Amal had tried to counter the initial attack on him, but he gave up after a particularly offensive comment was posted by someone on the team that he had regarded as a friend.

Amal's parents were unaware of what was going on. They noticed that he was not eating and seemed upset, but he was unwilling to talk to them. They thought this might just be part of normal teenage mood swings, but they became increasingly concerned when Amal refused to go to school the following week and missed football practice for the next two weeks. He kept looking at his phone, which seemed to be making him feel even worse, but was still not willing to share anything with his parents. The Team Coach, who was not aware of the group chat and had no idea what had happened, tried to encourage Amal back to training, but Amal refused.

Amal's Guidance Teacher noticed a change in his mood and general wellbeing when he returned to school following a week-long absence. She initially thought he might be recovering from a minor illness, but she noticed that he had detached from his usual friendship group and was spending more time alone at breaks and lunchtimes. The 'rumour mill' in school brought it to her attention that there was a rift between Amal and some of his football teammates who attended the same school. She interviewed one of these boys – he was open as to what had gone on, and he was also himself upset by some of the comments that had been made. She then spoke to Amal, and the full story was revealed. She was shown some of the comments, although Amal would not let her see everything that had been written about him.

Amal was given a self-referral card for the Base, to allow him some respite during the school day if he needed it, and he was encouraged to spend breaks and lunchtimes there in the short term, rather than just wandering around outside. With Amal's permission, his Guidance Teacher spoke to the PE Teacher, who happened to work alongside Amal's Team Coach with a younger team. They arranged to meet with Amal in the Base, to offer him the chance to discuss what had happened, and to resolve things.

Once the full details and extent of the bullying were revealed, the Coach held a special team meeting, without Amal being present, to establish clear rules around this kind of behaviour. It was made clear that anyone involved in this abuse was not welcome in the team, and that reparations had to be made. The main perpetrator was interviewed by the Coach and his place in the team put on the line until matters were fully resolved. Many of the other players were relieved that this matter had been dealt with, and they were keen to make full and unreserved apologies to their talented teammate.

Amal did return to the team for the rest of the season, but he did not join in any further group chat. Several other players also withdrew from it. Amal worked alongside his Coach to train a younger team until he was taken on for the following season by the club who had been following his progress.

Chapter 25: Peer pressure

Peer pressure and influence has a huge place in young people's lives. It is generally a positive force, giving young people a sense of enjoyment and belonging to a group. However, it can also wreak havoc when things go wrong – and changing a young person's chosen peer group is a very difficult thing to tackle. Parents and school staff tread a difficult path even to attempt it, and any efforts must be planned with great sensitivity, presented in a non-confrontational way and organised using a team approach.

> **Key Point**
>
> *Peer pressure is generally a positive force, giving a sense of enjoyment and belonging; however, it can wreak havoc when things go wrong.*

Peer influence is something we all experience as a normal part of our lives outside our immediate family groups. We do not always make what others might see as 'good choices' in our friendship groups, and schools, along with community and youth settings, are often the first places where damaging or inappropriate peer pressure negatively affects young people. Often, poor behaviour in school and deteriorating academic progress will bring problems with peer pressure to a head in the form of behaviour referrals or exclusion. The issue can also manifest itself outside school, and there may be concerns in the wider community regarding anti-social or offending behaviour.

Parents can seldom tackle problems with peer pressure unaided, and attempts to demonise other young people in their friends' eyes is more often counterproductive than helpful. It can lead to groups of young people being defined by their mistakes, and this in turn can lead to further disengagement, alienation and poor educational and social outcomes.

Secondary schools should always follow advice from primary schools about separating specific young people, and they should also separate pupils likely to adversely affect each other's behaviour and attainment when the time comes for subject choices and the formation of new classes. Pastoral care staff should identify friendship groups as pupils move through school, and monitor any behaviour or group influence on pupils that causes concern. The power and risks of peer pressure and influence should also be covered as part of PSHE or equivalent, with group discussion of issues encouraged.

Young people need to be supported in school to make sensible decisions and choices regarding friendship groups and peer pressure, and some individuals may require help to break away from a peer group without this leading to more problems. Enlisting senior pupils as 'peer educators' can often prove to be a supportive strategy that produces good results. Formal group work in school can be offered to pupils who would benefit from a greater understanding of group dynamics and behaviour management.

If concerns are identified and/or there is a deterioration in behaviour or attainment, then it is always best to work with the young people and their parents in a pupil-centred way to plan and agree the best way forward.

How to help – peer groups and peer pressure

- Be aware of who your child is socialising with, in and out of school. This may change when he or she moves to secondary school, matures and gains more independence. Encourage him or her to bring friends home, but try not to make judgements about them.

- Don't criticise your child's friends, attempt to influence his or her friendship group or try to ban him or her from seeing particular individuals. You will not succeed, and you may damage your relationship with your child for some time.

- Don't blame other young people for your child's behaviour without acknowledging your child's own responsibility. If there are concerns, these should be discussed, and an action plan agreed. This might involve referral to in-school or external supports.

- Engage the help of another trusted adult that your child has a good relationship with to support him or her independently.

- Be prepared for dealing with peer group issues to be a difficult, drawn-out process. Encourage your child to take up new interests. Spend more time with them, and keep speaking. Avoid turning conversations into confrontations, and avoid getting into heated arguments first thing in the morning or last thing at night.

Peer pressure case study 1: Harry

Harry's mother contacted his Guidance Teacher because she and her husband were at their wits' end. Harry had always been a lively boy, but he had a good relationship with his parents and his younger brother and sister and was particularly close to his paternal grandparents who lived nearby. He saw them on an almost daily basis, and they would take him on holidays.

Problems with Harry's behaviour at home manifested when he was fourteen and escalated to the point where his parents felt unable to cope. He was moody, uncommunicative and refused to follow any household rules. He had moved from being verbally abusive to being physically abusive – and his mother had called the police when he punched his father during an argument. His siblings were afraid of him, and his parents blamed his absolute attachment to his friends for his worsening behaviour and attitude to them.

In school, Harry's attainment had deteriorated but he still presented as a confident, well-mannered boy, albeit one with a short temper. He was a good rugby player and a pivotal member of the school team, both on and off the pitch. In a meeting with his mother and his Guidance Teacher, he admitted to often feeling out of control at home. He identified his group of friends as the single most important thing in his life, and he resented his parents trying to manage or restrict his contact with them.

Harry agreed a plan of action to support him both at home and in school. His Guidance Teacher met with his grandparents at his request, to support him further, and he was discussed as a priority at a school inter-agency meeting. It was agreed that in the short-term he would live with his grandparents but meet with his parents once a week for dinner. He was given a self-referral card for the Base, and offered anger management and youth worker support to tackle the home situation and his behaviour out of school. Social work support was put in place with the aim of repairing family relationships.

Harry struggled for some time to get everything back onto an even keel and to repair his relationship with his father, but eventually – with support from a number of key adults – he succeeded and returned home.

Peer pressure case study 2: Lucy

Lucy was in her third year at secondary school. Her older sister had been a pupil at the school, had left with respectable qualifications and had a job in hospitality at a large city hotel. However, Lucy was getting into trouble with staff for truancy, for failing to complete assignments and homework, and for being defensive when challenged about this. She had been excluded twice in her second year for verbal abuse of teachers. On a one-to-one basis, she got on well with staff and showed ability, but she seemed to be under the influence of a group of friends who had little interest in school and who also came into conflict with staff for low-level disruption and poor attainment.

Lucy had expressed an interest in training to be a Childminder or Nursery Teacher, but she was unlikely to be eligible for either of these because of her poor work attainment and the fact that she was in danger of further exclusion from school. Following a referral to her Guidance Teacher for an incident in Home Economics – her favourite class – Lucy was referred for one-to-one support in the Alternative Education Department to look at specific areas of concern, and to discuss how to improve matters.

Lucy readily agreed that she was unable to pull herself away from her friendship group, that this was what was adversely affecting her behaviour, and that she could see things escalating going forward. Several of her friends had been excluded in third year. She felt that it was just a matter of time before she was in the same position, which would affect her chances of being accepted for her chosen course at college.

The Education Welfare Officer (EWO) had been involved in trying to improve Lucy's attendance and to prevent truancy from school, and had worked alongside her Guidance Teacher to look at targets for the future. Lucy was discussed at the multi-agency Pupil Support Group. Hosting to another school was suggested as a strategy to give her a fresh start, to take her away from her peer group and to allow her to sit her national exams. Lucy's mother was in favour of this, but it was a harder decision for Lucy to make.

It was agreed that the Alternative Education Department Principal Teacher (who also coordinated hosting placements) would approach the other five schools involved in the hosting project to see if any of them had a space in third year, and whether they could offer Lucy the same subject choice. Everyone was keen for Lucy to attend a school where she had no existing friends or social contacts, and this immediately took two schools out of the mix. Two schools were able to offer a place, and visits were arranged to determine which would be more suitable in terms of travel, and which one felt best for Lucy and her mother. One of the schools immediately stood out as the better choice as it was on a direct bus route, quite near where Lucy's grandmother lived, and they could offer an almost perfect subject match.

After the initial eight-week trial period at the host school Lucy's class reports were much more positive, and she and her mother were pleased that things were going well. She had settled in easily, had established a good friendship group and had joined an extra-curricular sport club. She was offered a further eight-week trial or immediate enrolment, and she opted for the latter. She completed her school career in her new school and stayed on for sixth form – something that would have been unlikely in her original school.

Chapter 26: The 'quiet victim'

When working with young people experiencing long-term emotional problems such as family illness, separation, divorce or bereavement, it is always a good idea to engage with their closest friends too. Young people can quietly sink under the stress of being an emotional sponge for someone else's grief and pain, and engagement with those close to a distressed friend allows for parallel monitoring of their mood and welfare. This allows the young person to offload in a safe environment, and to know that his or her burden is recognised without it seeming like a betrayal of his or her friend.

> **Key Point**
>
> *Young people can quietly sink under the stress of being an emotional sponge for someone else's grief and pain.*

Similarly, when one member of a family is in crisis, this does not just affect the parent or parents; other siblings will also feel the impact of disputes, arguments and trauma, and they may resent the fact that everything can seem to focus on just one person – the person they see as the problem.

We disregard such 'quiet victims' at our peril. Trauma can wreck family relationships for many years to come through harboured resentment, and parents must not think that their other children are coping just because they do not share their feelings or distress. Everyone needs a voice in a family, not just the person who appears most in need or shouts the loudest.

The 'quiet victim' case study 1: Mia

Mia was one of the siblings of Harry (described in Chapter 25). She was in her first year at secondary school when he was in his third year, and when he was coming into almost daily conflict with his parents at home. Although Mia appeared to be coping well in school, she sometimes seemed distracted, and she had reported to the school nurse on several occasions with headaches and stomach pains. Her Guidance Teacher was aware of the older brother's issues at home – particularly his poor relationship with his father. She met with Mia to offer her the chance to offload, and to provide a level of support that recognised her needs as someone who was struggling to cope with frequent conflict and had recently witnessed physical violence.

Mia had good relationships with her brother and her parents, but she felt powerless when there was an argument raging in the house. She was afraid

Chapter 26: The 'quiet victim'

for her father and her brother, and for the impact that this was also having on her mother and younger siblings, who were openly distressed. She was initially reluctant to consider any sort of meeting about her welfare, although she did agree that the current situation was affecting her emotionally and that she was often left feeling anxious and unable to cope. She felt she could not add to her parents' burden, but ongoing staff concerns about her mood and a change in her academic achievement over the spring term prompted her to accept intervention on her behalf.

A pupil-centred meeting was held in school. Mia's parents, brother and grandparents were all invited to attend. A no-blame discussion was carefully managed by a sub-group of staff from the Pupil Support Group, and clear guidelines were set for her to have time in the Alternative Education Base (when her brother was not there). Specific strategies were agreed to give her an appropriate level of support in school on an 'as and when needed' basis.

Mia was given a self-referral card to the Base for respite or to allow her to access one-to-one support at short notice. She was also given a one-to-one support session each Monday morning to monitor how the weekend had been at home, and to settle her ready for the rest of the week (flash points at home had often been Friday and Saturday evenings).

When her brother moved out of the house to live with his grandparents, Mia went each Wednesday to have tea with him there so that they could catch up and maintain their positive relationship. This benefitted them both, and Mia felt that she was not having to choose which side she was on. Although the ongoing family situation was a long-term work in progress, things did improve for Mia quite rapidly, and she felt more settled and less anxious because she had a clear line of support and a chance to discuss and acknowledge the effects that all of this had had on her and her siblings.

The 'quiet victim' case study 2: Charlie and Ben

Charlie and Ben had been friends since primary school. They were in their fifth year at secondary school when Charlie's father was killed during a robbery while he was working abroad. The suddenness and violence of his death stunned the family, and the lack of information, media attention and delay in repatriating Charlie's father's body for burial made things even more difficult for them. The families were close friends, and the impact on them and their wider relatives was devastating.

Charlie had time off school, but he returned the week after his father's death. He did not want any additional support, avoided any questions or discussions about his father, and was protective of his mother, who was trying to deal with the Foreign Office and get through the red tape to repatriate her husband's body. Charlie's maternal grandparents lived nearby, and they had moved in with Charlie and his mother and younger sister, who was only six years old. His paternal grandparents lived abroad, but they were making plans to come to Britain as soon as possible.

Charlie and Ben were in most classes together at the time, and Ben was Charlie's main support. Ben was known to the Alternative Education team, as he volunteered in the department, and one of the Base teachers was also his English teacher. She noticed a change in his mood, and spoke to him at length about how he was coping not just with his own grief but also with Charlie's reliance on him. Ben was initially reluctant to admit that he was struggling. He felt that he was being disloyal to Charlie, and that he should be doing this without complaint, but it was too huge a task and he was finding it hard to keep going. He admitted to not sleeping, feeling anxious all the time and not getting any time to relax – or feeling guilty if he did. His work was suffering in school, and he had failed recent tests in key subjects.

Ben wanted to support Charlie, and he did not want to look even remotely like he was backing off, but he needed someone else to speak to beyond his parents and people who were upset. There were other people in the year group that he spoke to, but he felt that he couldn't share any of his feelings with them in case it looked like he was gossiping, or not being a good friend.

Charlie's Guidance Teacher had arranged for Charlie to get a self-referral card for the Alternative Education Base, to use as and when he wanted some space. He used it infrequently, but it was early days and he would have open access for the rest of his school career. It was agreed that Ben would also have a self-referral card, along with a regular one-to-one appointment with the Base teacher, who knew him well and could detect his mood without having to ask too much. He was over sixteen, so there were no confidentiality issues around any discussions, and he was free to say whatever he liked. He also had regular meetings with the male youth worker attached to the Base, who shared an interest in music and rugby. Their conversations could be more casual, but just as focused on supporting Ben.

An acknowledgement of the pressures that Ben was under was the key to managing this situation. Those individuals supporting people who are experiencing trauma need to be given the chance to offload, to be upset on their own behalf, and to look for ways to offer help to their friends or family without damaging themselves further. Otherwise, there is a danger of depression or mental health illness developing and going undetected. The Alternative Education Department was always sensitive to this, and included consideration of the 'quiet victim' as part of its everyday practice.

Chapter 27: Separation and divorce

Family issues are the root of many of the problems faced by young people, and they can prevent individuals from achieving their full potential at school. Single-parent and blended families do not in themselves pose any problem at all, and they can provide healthy, happy environments where children thrive. However, the stages of separation and divorce, and the bitter disputes that can occur between parents and families, can seriously affect young people.

> **Key Point**
>
> *Even if it comes as a relief for some young people when their parents separate, it does not alter the fact that it is a life-changing event.*

Even if it comes as a relief for some young people when their parents decide to separate, it does not alter the fact that it is a life-changing event. If the separation is unexpected then it can be devastating, and young people can experience similar responses as if they had suffered a bereavement. Having a network of support is crucial at this time, as the ability to manage the usual teenage stresses can easily be lost – leading to disengagement, alienation and a sense of insecurity. All of these can negatively impact attainment and wellbeing, and how well parents manage and negotiate these huge changes in family circumstances may determine much about how their children cope with all aspects of their lives at this most precarious of times.

Dealing with parents in new relationships and all that this can signify can be a minefield – particularly if a parent has left the family to be with someone else. It can throw up many problems that sometimes go unrecognised, and it can lead to open conflict, friction in the family and behaviour or attainment changes in school. If a parent subsequently remarries, or lives with a new partner in a long-term relationship, young people often find the prospect of stepparents, stepsiblings and a new household too much to cope with, and this can in some cases lead to feelings of abandonment and resentment. If new children are born into this family unit, then there should be careful consideration of older children, and reassurances should be given in a non-confrontational way to help them to cope with yet another layer of change.

Schools are usually notified by parents when a separation or divorce takes place, and all teachers of the pupil affected should be informed as a matter of course (though they should not seek to discuss the subject with him or her). Pastoral support should be offered on a one-to-one basis, and it should serve as the basis for any support agenda that follows. The young person should be given space and opportunity to vent his or her feelings in a safe environment. This can act like a pressure release valve, and it can help the young person to cope better in class afterwards.

The young person should be monitored, and any changes of behaviour or other issues investigated and addressed. Keep an eye on attainment and ability to meet deadlines. It is a good idea to check in with the young person on a Monday, as weekends are often the worst times and he or she may benefit from an extra chat on these days. Holidays can be another stress point, so the days leading up to a break (particularly Christmas, when the rest of the world seems happy) can be difficult times, and it can be useful for the young person to know that someone else acknowledges this.

Schools should engage equally with separated parents as far as possible, while accepting that full engagement with both parties may be impossible. It should be stressed to both parties that the young person is the priority, and that the school will not take sides. Contact should be maintained with the parent that the young person is staying with, but without excluding the other parent from receiving reports and other school information relating to his or her child – unless this has been ordered by a Court, or the pupil has asked for it specifically. There is an age of consent relating to Children's Rights in every Education Authority or equivalent, and this must be adhered to.

How to help – parental separation and divorce

 Be honest with your children. If your separation has been a long time in the making, it is unlikely to come as a total surprise. If it is sudden, you may not be able to deal with their questions and shock alongside your own. Engage the help of a trusted friend or family member to offer support to you and your children.

 Reassure your children that it is okay for them to have another adult to speak to. They may be too afraid of their feelings to ask the things they most want to know, and it's important that they can do so without feeling disloyal. They will be going through many of the same emotions as you, but they will often express them differently and at different times to different people.

- ☞ Plan what to say to your children and, as far as possible, stay calm and reassure them that, even if you are upset, you are going to work together to manage all the changes that will take place.

- ☞ Expect your children to be upset, even if they don't initially express this. They might be angry with you, your partner and the world in general. This is normal. Allow them to ask any questions and try to answer them honestly. Don't expect to have all the answers at the outset – there will be many discussions to iron out matters.

- ☞ Young people have opinions and often do take sides, but they shouldn't be expected to. Don't make them feel disloyal if they want to keep healthy relationships with both their parents. Don't use them to carry messages or to answer questions after a visit to the other parent. Don't expect them to cut off contact with the extended family (grandparents often suffer particularly badly in this situation) because of a dispute that is not of their making.

- ☞ Don't be tempted to criticise your ex-partner. Even if you feel personally entitled to loathe your ex-partner forever, your children should be allowed to have a healthy relationship with him or her.

- ☞ Don't allow other adults around you to criticise your ex-partner to your children. Don't have the same conversations about your break-up with your children as you might with your friends.

- ☞ Let your child's pastoral care teacher know that things have changed. Tell them you'll do this, and check whether they are happy for this to be spoken about. Often, children are okay for people to know, but prefer to leave it at that. It may help for a member of staff to act as a support, especially if it is close to exam time, or to get leeway for submission dates and deadlines.

- ☞ Don't discuss details of financial disputes, maintenance or intimate details of your break-up with your children. They should not be made party to this – it serves no valid purpose, it can worry them greatly, and it can adversely affect their relationship with the other parent (and also with you, if there is any retaliation).

Separation and divorce case study 1: Kara

Kara was in her fourth year of secondary school – a crucial year. She discovered that her father was having an affair because he was texting a woman using her phone. When Kara questioned her father, he refused to talk to her. She confided in an older, married sister who immediately told her mother. The family imploded, and Kara was instantly overwhelmed, trying to cope at home with her distraught mother and a younger sibling.

Kara's father moved to live with his new partner and her children, and he expected Kara to visit and be part of his new family. She struggled to do this, and she would agonise over being caught in the middle between two parents she loved (although she felt little respect for her father at this time). She would come to the Base for quiet time and one-to-one support – often at the start of the day if she hadn't had much sleep – and would discuss her feelings openly. She struggled when things became messy financially, and there was the added threat that she and her mother would lose their home.

Kara asked that her teachers be informed that she was going through a difficult time personally, but she did not want the specifics discussed. She was given leeway for work submission dates, and time in the Base during a non-examinable subject to catch up – or sometimes just to rest.

When Kara's father's new relationship broke down, he made overtures to her mother to be allowed back. Kara was completely opposed to this because of what she and her sibling had lived through for nearly six months. When Kara's mother relented and allowed him back into the home, Kara was unable to cope with the pretence that her life was back to normal. At one point, when she vented her anger, her father blamed her, saying that if she had kept quiet in the first place, things would have blown over and nobody would have been hurt. In many ways, this was an even harder thing for her to absorb and manage, and she felt that she was the person who had lost the most.

Kara continued to be supported until and throughout her final year in school, and she became a sixth-form Peer Volunteer. She was an excellent communicator with other young people who were experiencing family disruption, and she used her first-hand experience to help others. She left home after sixth form to take up a university place in another city.

Separation and divorce case study 2: Lewis

Lewis was a bright, articulate second year pupil who had nevertheless amassed so many punishments and exclusions that he was in danger of permanent exclusion. He would bait teachers, escalate low-level disruption into open verbal aggression, and disrupt learning for others.

Yet he was considerate and helpful towards other students, and many staff fought to keep him in their class because they liked him and felt that he was suffering emotionally. Their inability to manage him was frustrating, and neither sanctions nor normal Guidance support were effective in creating any change.

Lewis's parents were separating, but this was a lengthy and acrimonious process. He engaged well with both his mother and his father and did not take sides, but he found the situation at home extremely stressful and this had an impact on his behaviour at school. He was referred for one-to-one support and was allowed to self-refer to the Base to avoid confrontation with staff. This worked well, because teachers would prompt him to use this support when they could see him building up to a confrontation — or they would call the Base Teacher who could 'pop in' to the class to get him out on a pretext. Often, if he was wound up, they wouldn't talk but would play cards until he was calmer, or he would be given a task to do for the department.

In one-to-one discussion, Lewis was open about his frustrations at home, and could clearly identify the issues. He was being played off against both parents and had to listen to them criticising each other, and when they moved into separate houses he had to listen to complaints about financial settlements. He spent time in both his parents' houses, but he didn't feel very settled in either. The Base Teacher was in almost daily contact with both his parents, and this was a big factor in being able to address concerns honestly and openly. The teacher always made sure that Lewis knew what was being said and to whom, and she made it clear to all parties that he was the priority and that she would let him lead any further intervention.

The Base Teacher began to have concerns about Lewis's mental health when things became particularly stressful. He was taking increasing risks with his health and safety out of school, and advice was sought from Child and Adolescent Mental Health Services (CAMHS) about how best to support him as a matter of urgency. A referral was made to them for one-to-one support but in the interim, in negotiation with Lewis, one-to-one anger management and youth worker support was added immediately to his support package.

Over the next few weeks, Lewis reconnected with staff and built positive relationships. He took on roles of responsibility and excelled in several subjects, particularly practical ones where he could work with the minimum of supervision and show initiative. He was a young man who had to cope with much more than he should have had to, because of his parents' marital situation. The impact of this was significant, and without intensive support he could easily have become just another permanent exclusion statistic.

Chapter 28: Financial problems

Financial problems can have a significant impact on young people. Job insecurity and redundancy for parents affects their children, who may feel that they have less stability in their lives, and when a large local employer makes mass redundancies the impact on a school community can be immense. Financial problems can also stem from or lead to marital disputes.

> *Key Point*
>
> *Financial problems bring real concerns about the future for young people who are already dealing with a multitude of issues in their lives.*

These are very difficult times for families and, when schools are made aware of financial problems by parents or carers, any support should be offered as quickly and respectfully as possible. Young people are often more aware than their parents realise of family concerns about money and security, and the stresses that come from this. Financial problems bring real concerns about security and the future for young people who are already dealing with a multitude of transitional issues in their lives, while also juggling, schoolwork, friendships and the physical and emotional changes of adolescence.

Understandably, most people are protective of their family and their right to privacy, and do not want details of their personal circumstances – financial or otherwise – to be in the public domain. Any likelihood of parents informing schools of this most sensitive information will be dependent on them having good relationships with key staff, along with absolute trust that any support offered to the young person will be discreet.

Schools should be sure to include information about where parents can access additional financial support in the school handbook or prospectus, and on the school website. There should also be a school Hardship Fund, and staff should be made fully aware of how to access it quickly and sensitively for families in need. Pastoral care staff can also liaise with the Education Welfare Department (or equivalent) to source other possible grants/monies, and they can meet with parents or carers to discuss them and help with applications. Any discussion that takes place directly with the young person should be in a one-to-one setting, and the need for any other support should be determined and agreed with them at that stage.

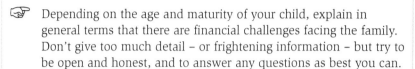

How to help – navigating financial difficulties

☞ Depending on the age and maturity of your child, explain in general terms that there are financial challenges facing the family. Don't give too much detail – or frightening information – but try to be open and honest, and to answer any questions as best you can.

☞ Explain the need to reduce allowances, treats or other additional expenses that your child may usually expect to receive, but do this in a structured way as part of a planned discussion, not as a spontaneous response to a request for money.

☞ If you have a good relationship with your child's or children's pastoral care teacher, inform them. There may be practical ways in which the school can help to cover the costs of lunches, fees for subject materials, uniform, school excursions and so on.

Financial problems case study 1: Daisy

Daisy's mother was a single parent who worked full-time. She and Daisy's father had been divorced for some years, amicably, and Daisy's father paid regular maintenance. Following the financial slump, Daisy's father was made redundant, and her mother also lost some hours at work. Daisy's mother contacted Daisy's Guidance Teacher to explain the situation.

Although the family was coping on a day-to-day basis, money was tight. Daisy had signed up for a school trip abroad, and the family had paid the deposit for it. Her mother was concerned that she would have to pull out. The Guidance Teacher spoke to the Head Teacher then to the School Bursar, and it was agreed that in order to allow Daisy to go on the school trip, the School Hardship Fund would cover the remaining cost. Daisy was not made aware of this, and no other staff were involved in the matter.

The Education Welfare Officer (EWO) also worked with Daisy's mother to check that she was receiving the correct benefits from the government. This was done at home, while Daisy was at school, and details of that work were confidential so there was no further discussion with the school.

Financial problems case study 2: Leah and Caitlin

Leah (in her second year) and Caitlin (in her third year) were sisters who enrolled in secondary school in January, after the term had started. They were placed in the Alternative Education Base full-time for a few days, to acclimatise them to the school and to allow Guidance staff to meet with them and arrange for class buddies to help them around. There was very little knowledge of their background, other than that they had been living in a Women's Refuge hostel in another town, and that they had only recently moved into rented accommodation in a run-down area near the school.

Leah refused to speak to staff, but would look to Caitlin to answer any questions for them both. The school learned that they had a younger brother (aged six) who had started at a local primary school that day, and that they had a baby sister at home with their mother. Their PPRs (Pupil Progress Records) had not yet reached the school, so staff had only patchy information to go by regarding previous schools and attainment levels.

Concern for the girls – and for the rest of the family – was immediate. They were clean but poorly dressed for the time of year, they appeared undernourished, and they had no money for lunches or bus fares. They left together at lunchtime, but staff were sure that they hadn't eaten anything when they returned for the afternoon. The Base was well stocked with healthy snacks and hot and cold drinks, so it was easy to provide them with something to eat. A sixth-form volunteer spent time with them, and the school Dining Hall Manager sent packed lunches made from leftover sandwiches until free school meals could be sorted out.

The Guidance Teacher for both girls contacted the Education Welfare Officer (EWO) to arrange an emergency home visit, and to find out what social work support was – or should be – in place. This visit was carried out the next day and, as a result, several supports were put in place for the family at home and for the girls in school. It transpired that the mother had experienced severe domestic violence, and this had resulted in mental health problems. With no family support in the area she was socially isolated and struggling to cope, but she was keen for her children to attend school. Financial problems were evident, and this was the priority for the family. She had been allocated a new social worker, but she had not met with him or her yet.

The EWO worked with Leah and Caitlin's mother to complete an application for emergency funding for household items and clothes for the children. The school provided the girls with sweatshirts, shirts and ties, and the nurse sourced winter jackets from friends with children who had outgrown them.

She also arranged for the girls to go through a bag of donated, good quality clothes including casual wear and shoes. The free school meal passes were rushed through the system, and the girls were issued with daily bus passes.

The girls spent two weeks full-time in the Base until all these provisions were in place. It was agreed that Caitlin would go into the Reduced Timetable Social Skills Group, so that she could benefit not only from practical aspects of the course but also from the one-to-one attention and support from the teacher who managed it. Caitlin was bearing much of the burden of looking after the family, and she needed some respite from this responsibility. In the Base, she could offload to teachers but also do more fun, creative activities that she had missed out on as a child. Her mother was encouraged to come into school to meet the girls at the end of the day, and she got to know the Base staff well. This was useful for everyone, and the girls enjoyed showing their mother how well they were doing.

The Base staff liaised with all teaching departments in the school to make the girls' transition to classes easier. All material costs for practical subjects were paid from the school fund. The EWO worked closely with the local primary school to ensure that all necessary supports were in place for their younger brother, and further liaison took place with the local nursery when their baby sister was enrolled there a few weeks later.

While the most immediate practical and financial issues were relatively straightforward and easy to sort out, this was a family with complex needs that would only be met by a multi-agency approach over many years.

Chapter 29: Bereavement and loss

It is a sad fact that a significant number of pupils in any school will have to deal with the death of someone close to them during their school career. Bereavement is often the underlying issue for other problems that manifest in attendance, behaviour and mental health concerns. The death of a loved grandparent who may have been a regular child-minder, carer and friend is a considerable loss for a young person, whose sadness can be overshadowed by the grief of parents. However, the loss of a parent, sibling or someone their own age can be simply devastating, and it requires an even greater awareness of the young person's journey through the grieving process.

> **Key Point**
>
> It is a sad fact that a significant number of pupils in any school will have to deal with the death of someone close to them during their school career.

Where a death is not unexpected, there may have been some preparation and support in advance of the loss. This does not make things easier, just different. The sudden death of a pupil or member of staff, from an accident, illness or suicide, has a significant impact on the whole school. Schools should have a plan of action in place as part of their policy for dealing with this, to support pupils and staff. This could involve class, year or whole school assemblies, and perhaps an in-school service or some sort of permanent memorial. Members of the school community should have access to professional counselling services if they require them. If some pupils wish to attend a funeral then this should be supported, and pastoral care staff should accompany any pupils who are not with their parents.

Pastoral care for bereaved pupils should be provided in much the same way as for other forms of trauma and upset – with one-to-one support offered and the young person allowed to decide what form, if any, this should take. Class teachers should be informed – especially in subjects where death or dying might come up, and where affected young people may prefer to opt out of such discussions. Respite facilities should be provided for vulnerable times, with no time limit imposed and monitoring in place should further support or referral to outside agencies be required. As always, schools must be away that other members of their community will be helping to support a bereaved person, and that they may also need help to cope with this.

How to help – coping with bereavement and loss

☞ Inform the school as soon as possible of a bereavement, even an expected one, to allow pastoral care staff time to provide appropriate support for your child in school.

☞ Explain as much as you can to your child, or ask a trusted adult to do it if you can't, and be prepared for questions. It is better to know that a parent doesn't have all the answers, or is finding it hard to cope, than to be excluded or left in the dark.

☞ Allow your child to be upset, angry and afraid, but don't worry if he or she seems to carry on as normal. People react differently, and the full impact might not be felt immediately. Be prepared for the possibility of disruption to your child's sleep patterns and/or mood swings. Keep to a routine, and try to talk about any mood problems when he or she is calm and able to discuss things.

☞ Give your son or daughter a choice about attending the funeral. Don't make that decision for them, and let them change their mind. Allow them to take part in or contribute to the funeral if they wish to, but don't apply any pressure to do this. Have another adult ready to step in to support your child on the day if required.

☞ Your son or daughter may seem preoccupied with death or dying and appear almost insensitive to your feelings. Make time to listen and talk – when you feel able to cope with this. If they become anxious and fearful that other people will die, offer reassurance and encourage them to be with friends to normalise their life.

☞ If the death was expected and palliative care was in place, there will be support available for family members. Young people often appreciate being able to access this in the months after their loss. If the death was a suicide, be ready for added layers of emotions, reactions and questions that may never be fully answered.

☞ Keep to regular mealtimes, don't skip meals, and eat together. Ensure your child takes part in some physical exercise – even if it's just a walk. Encourage him or her to keep attending any sports clubs, but inform the leader or coach of what has happened.

Watch for signs of depression – changes in patterns of behaviour and disengagement from usual routines and friendship groups. Approach a discussion about your concerns gently, but don't be fobbed off if you think this could be an issue. Suggest seeking help – don't just arrange something without prior discussion.

 Contact bereavement agencies if you feel that your child is not coping after some time has elapsed. Grief is a process and cannot be rushed, but sometimes people get 'stuck' and need help to get through this stage. Some counselling agencies are directed at young people. They can be thin on the ground, but your GP or your child's pastoral care teacher may be able to direct you.

Bereavement and loss case study 1: Charlotte and Oliver

Charlotte and Oliver were respectively in their fourth and fifth year at secondary school. After their mother was diagnosed with a terminal illness, she and her husband informed the school and asked for a meeting with the Guidance Teacher who worked with both young people. It was agreed that Charlotte and Oliver would be referred to the Alternative Education Base. They were immediately given intensive, one-to-one support along with self-referral cards allowing them access to the Base whenever they needed it. Each chose to attach to a different member of staff, which gave them a degree of control and allowed them to receive individual, tailored support.

Teaching staff were made aware of their situation, and they supported Charlotte and Oliver in terms of workload and submission dates for assessments. Both pupils' timetables were reduced – taking them out of non-examinable areas – to allow them study time to concentrate on their academic work, and to give them a quiet area in school. Guidance and Base staff met with their parents, who were keen to discuss the support they knew their daughter and son would need now and into the future.

As their mother's condition deteriorated (she remained at home), the school became more flexible around start and finish times for Charlotte and Oliver. Sometimes, one of them would come to the Base to catch up on sleep for an hour or two during the day. Following their mother's death, both pupils were supported through the rest of their school careers, and contact was maintained after they left. Both went to university to do teaching degrees.

Bereavement and loss case study 2: Ruby

Ruby and several of her friends needed support following the suicide of a girl in their group. There had been no indication that the girl was depressed or not coping, so the ramifications for the group of girls were immense. There was huge public and media interest in their friend's death. Blame was attached to some of the members of the girls' group by other teenagers, and shock waves went through the whole school community.

The school held a year group assembly to inform pupils and to offer support. Individual Guidance Teachers supported some pupils on a one-to-one and small-group basis. The Head Teacher and Guidance Teacher for the girl who had died had contact with her parents. The immediate concern, though, was for the group of friends – and in particular for Ruby, who was felt to be at risk of serious self-harm.

It was decided that the Base team would work to support these girls in school. They liaised with Psychological Services for the local authority to agree strategies. The girls were not allowed to go to their friend's funeral, so a small, personal gathering was arranged in the Base while the funeral was taking place, and the girls asked Base staff to approach the School Chaplain to lead this. They brought photographs, and each girl spoke about their friend and how they felt. The next day, staff from the Base took them as a group to the cemetery to lay flowers, and later they worked with them on a small, personal memorial.

As the death had been investigated by the police, the Base managed to set up a three-session group meeting, which consisted of the investigating police officer, a group social worker, the girls, and the Head of the Base. The girls asked very specific questions about their friend, and the police officer took note of these and answered them at the next meeting. This was very sensitive, intense and traumatic work – but it was invaluable for the girls.

For Ruby, it was a long process, and she struggled more than the rest of the group. She was already self-harming, and she was considered to be at serious risk of suicide. She was referred for one-to-one social work and Bereavement Counselling as a priority, and she continued with Base support so that she could access help outside the school day and term time. She continued to be supported after she left school to take up employment.

Chapter 30: Young carers

Any young person who lives in a household where they are involved in the daily care of an adult or other siblings due to illness (physical or mental) or dependency (drugs, alcohol, etc.) issues can be described as a young carer.

> **Key Point**
>
> *Any young person who lives in a household where they are involved in the daily care of an adult or other siblings can be described as a young carer.*

Young carers have different lives to other young people. They are often involved in providing personal support – washing, dressing or feeding someone, or taking on parenting tasks to allow the family to survive. They can also be the ones who manage the household budget, do the shopping and liaise with landlords and other agencies in the place of their parent.

Young carers often bear a huge weight of responsibility, and although they might manage this well, they are not on a level playing field with their peers in terms of being able to act like other teenagers. They can seldom socialise with their friends, may not be able to invite people to their home and can feel particularly isolated at weekends and during school holidays. They may appear mature, but this early maturity can come at a cost for their educational attainment and emotional welfare, and it can restrict their freedom of choice regarding post-school education or employment.

It is important for parents to recognise the extent to which their child takes on this role in the family, and also to make this clear to the school. This will allow every available support to be put in place for the young person, and ensure that the family receives all the outside agency help it is entitled to.

In Britain, young people caring for another person in their family can be referred by any agency to the Young Carers Organisation – which offers one-to-one, peer and family support along with respite activities for young people. This might be as simple as a youth group meeting after school or during holidays, or it may involve more intensive family support. Other similar organisations will be available in different regions, and GPs, social work and children and families teams will be aware of them. An online search should also flag up local resources and helpful websites.

Schools can offer support to young carers once they are identified, just as they would for any young person facing exceptional family circumstances. One-to-one pastoral care support for young carers is vitally important, and they should be given additional time, provided with self-referral cards to a respite area, and be known individually to the school nurse. Just being aware that an adult in the school understands their issues and can negotiate with the other staff on their behalf is a huge weight off their minds.

Young carers case study 1: Yusuf

CYusuf lived with his parents and three younger siblings. His parents had moderate learning difficulties, and they relied on Yusuf to manage many routine household tasks – including paying bills, liaising with the Housing Department regarding building repair and maintenance issues, and sorting out any other problems that they couldn't manage or which overwhelmed them at times. Yusuf was a pleasant, engaging pupil with an enthusiastic attitude to school. He was well regarded by staff and other pupils in his year group, but his punctuality was problematic from early on in his first year.

Although Yusuf's home situation was well documented from primary school, there was no record of ongoing support from any external agency. The family seemed to be coping reasonably well and there was no evidence whatsoever of emotional or physical neglect (the children were well dressed and well nourished), but it became evident to the Guidance Teacher that Yusuf was bearing much of the load for the family's care, and this was only increasing as all the children got older. There had been social work involvement with the family in previous years when Yusuf was in primary school and when he only had one other sibling, but this had been removed following a series of financial cuts to the department, and because the family were not regarded as a high priority for support or intervention.

Yusuf's parents were caring and loving, but they relied heavily on supportive family and good neighbours. As Yusuf moved into the upper school, he was regarded as the person who could best represent his parents. He began to attend his siblings' primary parents' evenings, then took on responsibility for managing the family budget for anything beyond food shopping. His Guidance Teacher flagged up concerns when she learned that he had missed a morning at school to visit the Housing Department to try to sort out a rent arrears issue which his parents could not deal with.

Yusuf's Guidance Teacher contacted his parents, who were open and honest about their reliance on their oldest child. They were keen for this to be discussed at the Pupil Support Group to see if other agencies could be brought in to support them, to release Yusuf from some responsibility and allow him just to be a child again. They were happy to attend this meeting, and they asked a family friend to attend in a supportive capacity.

The Pupil Support Group agreed several strategies to support Yusuf, his parents and his siblings:

- There would be an immediate referral to social work for an assessment of the family situation, and to agree appropriate support.
- Other adults in the extended family would be contacted by the parents to request support until agencies could respond (there were local family members who were known to be reliable and accessible).
- The Education Welfare Officer would become involved in supporting the family immediately to help the younger children get to school on time, and to allow Yusuf to start his day with less pressure.
- Yusuf would receive one-to-one support from the in-school youth worker to monitor his situation, and to offer him additional personal support until family supports were in place.
- Yusuf was referred to Young Carers to offer him groupwork, respite and social activities. A separate referral was made for his siblings, but they attended different activities so that Yusuf had more free time and could feel that he had something that was just for him.

Things moved quickly for the family once the social work referral was picked up as a matter of urgency. Yusuf enjoyed his activities with the Young Carers, and he thrived in school when he felt he had the time just to focus on his work and not feel the burden of responsibility for the whole family. The Young Carers organisation supported him throughout his time at school.

Young carers case study 2: Molly

Molly's situation as a young carer was well documented. She lived with her mother and her disabled sister, who attended a city school for pupils with physical disabilities. Although there were supports in place for her mother, and Molly was managing well in school, there were concerns that everything at home revolved around her sister's care and needs (she required help with mobility, eating and personal care). Molly was close to her sister, and had a good relationship with her mother, but she felt that she was unable to bring friends home and that she needed to be on hand more to support her sister and her mother. She was missing out on social contact with her peers, and sometimes appeared tired in school if her sister had had a disturbed night.

There was already social work support in place for the family, but it was agreed that more could be done to support Molly individually. She was discussed at a Pupil Support Group meeting (with her mother and her social worker present) and the following action points were agreed:

- Molly would have one-to-one support from the in-school youth worker attached to the Alternative Education Base.

- She would be issued with a self-referral card to use if she'd had a bad night at home – to allow her to have a break, or to sleep if needed.
- She would be referred to the Young Carers organisation – for individual support and for social activities groupwork.
- Molly's mother would get respite support once a week on a set day, to establish a routine and allow her and Molly to do things together.
- An application was made to a charity offering supported breaks for families including a person with physical needs. This was successful, and the family had their first holiday together for ten years in a supported environment where everyone could relax.
- Molly's mother would help Molly to create a private social area in her bedroom where she could bring her friends, where she would not be interrupted and where her friends could stay over.

Molly's situation improved quickly because most of these provisions could be implemented without much difficulty or effort. It freed up time for everyone, and having a regular structure to the week helped them all to cope better. Molly's social life was more rewarding, and her mood in school improved markedly because she felt she had more freedom to put herself first from time to time.

Part 6: Conclusion

Chapter 31 – Summary

This chapter recaps on the many factors covered in this book that relate to the nature, prevalence, identification and management of teenage school difficulties. Recognising the circumstances and situations that can make it hard for young people to cope in the melting pot of secondary education during their adolescent years enables those involved in shaping an individual's experiences, both at home and in school, to provide more effective support. Ideal outcomes are not always possible, but an understanding of the issues involved, and knowledge of the best strategies to adopt when seeking to tackle such issues, are positive and effective steps towards making the secondary school years a rewarding experience for all involved.

> **Key Point**
>
> *Recognising the circumstances and situations that make it hard for young people to cope enables those involved to provide more effective support.*

Give the young person a voice

It is important to listen carefully to a troubled young person, to allow them space to be angry or upset, and not to make assumptions about what might be upsetting them. Adults should use open questioning to encourage a process of reflection and dialogue, and they should acknowledge the seriousness of any issues that may surface during this process. Discuss these issues in depth, don't minimise their importance from an adult perspective, and don't offer generic advice or meaningless platitudes.

See the young person as an individual

Young people are unique individuals, each with their own issues and needs, and there are no easy, one-size-fits-all answers when it comes to resolving the difficulties that they may experience at secondary school. We have stressed our guiding approach that effective support of children and young people who are struggling with teenage school difficulties means tailoring help to the individual – which means adapting discussions, support and interventions to the young person's character, history and personality.

Put the young person at the centre

The best way to approach teenage school difficulties is always to keep the young person at the centre of everything. Whatever the challenges being experienced, the overriding aim is to give the individual the freedom to be himself or herself, the opportunity to experience success and the means to develop resilience. Sometimes a young person will not be aware that they need help; in other situations, for example in cases of bullying, they might not wish for action to be taken. The sooner problems of this kind are faced and addressed, the greater the likelihood of young people overcoming their difficulties and being able to cope as healthy adults. So working with the young person's preferences is essential at all stages of the journey.

Consider the young person's wellbeing

Young people today are much more aware of issues of mental health and wellbeing than their forbears, and as a result the stigma associated with such issues is much reduced from levels of the past. However, children do not always have the emotional maturity to understand and articulate the source of their distress. Schools must be notified of any additional support needs that a young person may have, and kept up to date with any change of circumstances that is likely to have an impact on health, wellbeing or welfare. There should also be a good supervision system within the school for staff to share any concerns about children in their care.

Provide a safe environment

Pastoral care in an educational context means ensuring the physical and emotional safety of pupils in school, and linking this to a secure and supportive home environment. With such provisions in place, all children and young people are given the opportunity to enjoy high levels of wellbeing and to perform to their full potential. Clear discussion of Child Protection Guidelines should take place early in each pupil's school journey, in order to make young people aware of limits enforced at a national level as well as those specific to the school. Teachers, in common with all professionals working with young people, must be fully aware of Child Protection legislation and their obligation to deal with all disclosures in accordance with it.

Provide time and space for cooling off

Young people experiencing teenage school difficulties may require the means to remove themselves from situations that are likely to trigger issues. A designated area for those requiring extra support, such as the Alternative Education Base in the case study school, can offer a space for respite and reflection with trusted staff members on hand to provide assistance if required. Such a facility offers a positive alternative to disaffection, exclusion and/or truancy, and it allows the young person to continue with academic work outside class. While they should be used with care, self-referral passes offer a degree of control and allow young people to self-manage this aspect of their emotional journey.

Consider siblings...

When a family experiences a crisis, it has an impact on everyone – not just the young person directly affected and the parent or parents. Brothers and sisters will be upset by arguments and trauma, and they may resent the fact that everything can seem to revolve around the person they see as the root of the problem. If a sibling attends the same school as the person experiencing difficulties, then their wellbeing should also be monitored and support offered if necessary. Respite can be made available to them, too, allowing the opportunity to process feelings in a safe space with help on hand.

...and friends

Fellow pupils are also vulnerable if a young person experiences difficulties and turns to close friends for support. If a young person approaches a member of staff to share concerns for a friend's wellbeing, this information should be acted on quickly and sensitively. However, it is easy to overlook pupils who are helping a friend to cope with a known issue. Anxiety for another individual's wellbeing is a heavy burden for anyone to carry, but often young people will not seek help for fear of betraying a confidence or letting their friend down. Any intervention must therefore be handled very sensitively, with maintaining the friendship of paramount importance.

Collaboration is key

Parents should work in collaboration with school staff to support their child. They should notify the school of any additional support needs, and keep staff informed of any change of personal circumstances that may have an impact on wellbeing, behaviour or attainment in school. Early intervention is critical to effective support, but it must be a two-way process between school and home. For parents and carers, whose greatest fear may be that a child will be removed from their care, it is important to have faith in authority and to have confidence in disclosing and discussing problems. Positive relationships and mutual trust are always the surest foundation for success.

> **Key Point**
>
> Early intervention is critical to effective support, but it must be a two-way process between school and home.

Take a whole-school approach to wider issues

The most effective way to tackle teenage school difficulties at the broadest level is by adopting a whole-school approach to issues of trauma, mental health, pupil wellbeing and emotional and social development – that is, by embedding understanding and skills related to these areas within staff training, the daily school routine and outward to ongoing partnerships with parents and the wider local community. Schools should aspire to a culture where young people feel included, respected and secure, where their achievements and contributions are valued and celebrated, and where there is a focus on positive relationships across the whole school community.

Consider community sources of support

Good provision of pastoral care requires well-developed liaison with the local community and all other relevant agencies. Within the case study school, the Pupil Support Group included a community police officer who was also involved in working with pastoral care staff to deliver bullying information as part of PSHE classes. Youth workers, community workers, psychologists, social workers and Education Welfare Officers (EWOs) can all become part of the wider school family, although much of the work they do may need to remain confidential within Child Protection guidelines. Later, community groups can provide opportunities for volunteering, work experience and vocational-based training, enhancing employability for young people.

Consider the cause of the behaviour or feelings

Problematic behaviour in the classroom, whether disruptive or withdrawn, can be a symptom of deeper problems in a young person's life outside school. Indeed, many 'difficult' pupils are those who have faced, or are facing, wider problems, and they need support to make sense of their world. Teenage school difficulties can seldom be taken at face value, and issues of friendship dynamics, problems at home, transition trauma and more can often be at the root of problems. Staff should be alert to subtle, as well as more obvious, signs that something is wrong, and ready to investigate possible causes for changes in behaviour, mood, attendance or general wellbeing.

Take a non-punitive approach

Approaches to tackling teenage school difficulties should be non-punitive wherever possible, and in cases where more than one pupil is involved care should be taken to avoid apportioning blame. A non-punitive approach avoids stigma and allows for constructive working toward solutions. It is important to gain pupil trust, and for any intervention to be seen as supportive rather than corrective or suggestive of failure or deficit on the pupil's part. Where punishment around behaviour is appropriate as part of the school discipline policy, it should be matched with a collaborative, restorative approach.

Make and agree a practical plan

For an intervention designed to overcome issues or challenge negative behaviours to be successful there must be good cooperation, open and honest dialogue, and shared responsibility to try to effect change. The young person must be kept at the centre of the conversation and allowed to be in control so that the plan is one he or she can agree to – otherwise, it will fail. Parents should be involved as much as possible, and a positive, realistic course of action should be agreed along with a timescale for reviews. Progress should be monitored, and new goals set regularly. If no improvement has been seen after an agreed period, consideration can be given to more far-reaching strategies such as the young person moving to another school.

Be creative and open to change

When planning interventions and solutions, be creative and innovative. Think of what might work in a best-case scenario, then work towards that goal. Each individual is unique, and each case must therefore be handled individually and on its own merits. So a bespoke approach, within the parameters of general guidelines, is often more effective than trying to use a catch-all method. Be creative too in thinking about forms of support and drawing on resources such as external agencies and community links. Always be prepared to tear up a plan and start again.

Build strengths and promote resilience

Dealing with teenage school difficulties is critical for two key reasons – to improve the wellbeing of the young person in the short term, and to help them build resilience for the long term. Mental health issues are easier to address in youth than in later life, and tackling such problems quickly rather than allowing them to take root increases the likelihood of individuals being able to cope well as adults. Conversely, tactics such as truancy that seek to avoid the issue can hinder the development of resilience and should always be discouraged. Approaches and interventions should always be positive, pupil-centred, and designed to provide young people with the opportunity to experience success. Issues that are not acknowledged or properly managed can lead to a raft of problems in later years, and investment in preventative work in childhood and adolescence is always money well spent.

Help to manage emotions

Young people can experience a wide range of stresses, issues and difficulties as they cope with the simultaneous demands of adolescence and secondary education, and all of them are like to have an impact on short-term wellbeing and educational performance. Because young people lack emotional experience, it is critical that parents, carers, teachers and schools identify warning signs and provide early support wherever appropriate. Discussions should always be focused on generating dialogue and encouraging the young person to open up and explain what his or her perceptions are. Remember that those closest to young people and their issues are not always the best placed to provide help, and in some cases it can be of great benefit to bring in another trusted adult to help with objectivity and reassurance.

Break cycles of behaviour

Issues of the kind that we have discussed in this book, if left unaddressed, can easily develop into unhelpful patterns of behaviour. Whether it be something as apparently trivial as classroom disruption due to lack of motivation, or as serious as ongoing self-harm, once established these patterns become very hard to break. It is for this reason that, as we have stressed repeatedly, early intervention is critical when seeking to manage teenage school difficulties. Effective early intervention tackles problems before they get worse, boosts protective factors while managing risk factors, and helps foster skills and strengths that will last young people a lifetime.

Chapter 32 – A last word to parents and carers

Many people worry about their child's future, but they do not always think about their child's present life, health and well-being. A great piece of advice for any parent who wants their child to do well, succeed and be happy over the long term is to look closely at what is happening now. That is what will shape your child's future. Don't ignore a serious problem and hope that it will go away; almost certainly it won't. Unresolved issues often resurface when something else goes wrong, and young people can then easily get caught up in feelings of helplessness and resentment. As we have noted, problems are often more easily treated in young people than in adults.

> **Key Point**
>
> *A great piece of advice for any parent who wants their child to succeed and be happy over the long term is to look at what is happening now.*

As well as being honest with yourself about problems that may exist, do not be tempted to hide potential issues from your child's school if you feel that they may have an impact on his or her attitude, behaviour or attainment. Schools deal with teenagers every day, and they will not judge you for not coping; you are not alone in this! The sooner a school knows that there are circumstances to consider or factors to take account of when teaching and interacting with a young person, the sooner they can help. Furthermore, a failure to be open and collaborative can lead to a breakdown of the parent-school relationship, to the detriment of your child. So put your faith in authority, trust that the right expertise and resources will be called upon, and give your child the best possible chance of addressing his or her teenage school difficulties, overcoming them and flourishing in the long term.

If times get tough, remember that there are other people and organisations who can offer you good advice and support, based on grounded experience of working with young people. Most have a website that you can visit, and this is often the first step to getting support for yourself and for your child. So ask for help when you need it from friends who know you and your child, and who may be able to mediate, offer suggestions, or be a sounding board. Seek help from your GP, who can investigate medical problems and suggest referrals to other agencies. And explore resources in the wider community; there are several parent forums where advice is available and support networks are advertised. You can chat to other parents who have similar experiences, and who may have suggestions for practical help.

Keep in mind at all times that being a parent is a difficult task! Congratulate yourself when things go well and you get it right, but don't beat yourself up when things go wrong. As parents or carers, you are not expected to have all the answers all the time – and you will not be judged for that.

Chapter 33 – A last word to teachers and schools

Secondary school teachers are employed principally to instruct pupils in a subject. However, this is only part of the job. Newly qualified teachers will find themselves responsible for the care and welfare of many young people, and at times this can be emotionally draining. Within a class of pupils, of any age, there will be a range of learning needs but also different social, emotional, family and personal issues that affect health, wellbeing and academic performance. This can be stressful, but support is available – for example experienced teachers to learn from and classroom observation to help with self-evaluation. So don't be afraid to ask for advice; we never stop learning, and we all need to tap into the skills and strengths of others so that we can offer the best possible service to the young people in our care.

> **Key Point**
>
> *We all need to tap into the skills and strengths of others so that we can offer the best possible service to the young people in our care.*

Schools should encourage an atmosphere of collegiate learning and use the staff team's talents well. Senior management will be aware of which teachers can inspire pupils, and which can manage discipline, and should use them to provide good quality in-house training. Non-judgemental support should be offered to any colleagues who are struggling to cope, as this could be for personal as well as professional reasons and schools have a duty of care to staff as well as pupils. Consider sharing specialist skills with other schools in the area – there might be a possibility for two school to be able to fund and staff creative project work for a targeted group of vulnerable young people, where one school could not manage to do so alone.

Parents of pupils can also be a valuable resource. Many of them will have the skills and time to help support projects in school. This can be anything from speaking to pupils about careers to getting involved (after appropriate checks) with subject departments and the pupil support team to collaborate on specific projects. Celebrate the success of all work that promotes the long-term health and wellbeing of young people. Support departments are often soft targets for cuts and although all departments can make cases for funding, it is important that the support of pupils with social, emotional, family and personal problems is also seen as a priority. Young people must not be marginalised at a time when they are wholly depending on schools to recognise their needs and to support them appropriately.

Finally, it is crucial to look after the whole person, in context. Parents and schools share much of the responsibility for educating young people to fulfil their academic potential, but an important additional responsibility is to encourage independent thought, to develop resilience and confidence, and to celebrate diversity and a respect for others. Young people need to feel a sense of purpose, that their skills and uniqueness are important, and that they are valued and have a place in the world. They are the future, and we must support them during the crucial years of their development. With care and patience, we will also improve their education in the broadest sense.

Index of *How to Help* advice

Supporting your child at primary school	26
How schools can support children and families	28
Warning signs of distress for parents and carers	33
Warning signs of distress for teachers and schools	34
Warning signs of distress for friends	35
A parent's guide to secondary school transition	38
Transition tactics for teachers and schools	39
Assisting with organisation	44
Adapting to increased workload	50
Advising on subject choice	54
Managing disengagement	59
Preventing disengagement in schools	60
Minimising truancy and absenteeism	67
Tackling school refusal	72
Planning for life beyond school	76
Adjusting to illness and disability	82
Sharing mental health concerns	86
Harnessing the power of self-esteem	90
A positive approach to sexual health	96
Eating disorder warning signs	102
Identifying and managing eating disorders	104
Recognising and managing self-harm	111
Confronting dependency	116
Friendship groups and issues	126
Addressing bullying problems	131
Promoting online safety	136
Peer groups and peer pressure	142
Parental separation and divorce	150
Navigating financial difficulties	156
Coping with bereavement and loss	160

Index of case studies

Secondary transition case study 1: Megan and Ella 40
Secondary transition case study 2: Cameron and Jake 41
Organisation case study 1: Tom 44
Organisation case study 1: Scarlett 45
Increased workload case study 1: Phoebe 51
Increased workload case study 2: Zak 51
Subject choice case study 1: Hannah 55
Subject choice case study 2: Ethan 55
Disengagement case study 1: Aaron 61
Disengagement case study 2: Fourth year girls 62
Absenteeism case study 1: Freya 67
Absenteeism case study 2: Kyle 68
School refusal case study 1: Jacob 73
School refusal case study 2: Emma 74
Post-school options case study 1: Rhys 77
Post-school options case study 2: Florence 77
Illness and disability case study 1: Isabelle 83
Illness and disability case study 2: Dylan 84
Mental health case study 1: Lily 87
Mental health case study 2: Noah 87
Self-esteem case study 1: Isla 90
Self-esteem case study 2: Liam 91
Sexual health case study 1: Matthew 97
Sexual health case study 2: Fourth year pupils 98
Eating disorders case study 1: Ellie 105
Eating disorders case study 2: Grace 106
Self-harm case study 1: Amelia 112
Self-harm case study 2: Fredek 113
Dependency case study 1: Ryan 118
Dependency case study 2: Amy 119
Friendships case study 1: Emily 126
Friendships case study 2: Daniel 127
Bullying case study 1: William 131
Bullying case study 2: Jessica 132
Cyberbullying case study 1: Lauren 137
Cyberbullying case study 2: Amal 138

Peer pressure case study 1: Harry 143
Peer pressure case study 2: Lucy.. 143
The 'quiet victim' case study 1: Mia... 145
The 'quiet victim' case study 1: Charlie and Ben................................ 146
Separation and divorce case study 1: Kara.. 152
Separation and divorce case study 2: Lewis 152
Financial problems case study 1: Daisy 156
Financial problems case study 2: Leah and Caitlin 157
Bereavement and loss case study 1: Charlotte and Oliver 161
Bereavement and loss case study 1: Ruby... 162
Young carers case study 1: Yusuf 164
Young carers case study 1: Molly 165

References

Attwood, G. & Croll, P. (2006) Truancy in secondary school pupils: prevalence, trajectories and pupil perspectives, Research Papers in Education, 21:4, 467-484, DOI: 10.1080/02671520600942446

Bronfenbrenner, U. (1977) Toward an experimental ecology of human development. American Psychologist, 32 (7): 513-531

Glover, D, Gough, G., Johnson, M. & Cartwright, N. (2000) Bullying in 25 secondary schools: incidence, impact and intervention, Educational Research, 42:2, 141-156, DOI: 10.1080/001318800363782

Haydn, T. (2014), To what extent is behaviour a problem in English schools? Exploring the scale and prevalence of deficits in classroom climate. Rev Educ, 2: 31-64. doi:10.1002/rev3.3025

Kearney, C. A. & Bates, M., Addressing School Refusal Behavior: Suggestions for Frontline Professionals, Children & Schools, Volume 27, Issue 4, October 2005, Pages 207–216, https://doi.org/10.1093/cs/27.4.207

O'Connor, R., Rasmussen, S., Miles, J., & Hawton, K. (2009). Self-harm in adolescents: Self-report survey in schools in Scotland. British Journal of Psychiatry, 194(1), 68-72. doi:10.1192/bjp.bp.107.047704

Smink, F.R.E., van Hoeken, D. & Hoek, H.W. Curr Psychiatry Rep (2012) 14: 406. https://doi.org/10.1007/s11920-012-0282-y

Spratt, J., Shucksmith, J., Philip, K. & Watson, C. (2006) 'Part of Who we are as a School Should Include Responsibility for Well-Being': Links between the School Environment, Mental Health and Behaviour, Pastoral Care in Education. 24 (3): 14-21 https://doi.org/10/1111/j.1468-0122.2006.00374.x

Westwood, J. & Mullan, B. (2006) Knowledge of secondary school pupils regarding sexual health education, Sex Education, 6 (2): 151-162

DOI: 10.1080/14681810600579121